WAYMISH

The People Who've Read It Say . . .

"As we fast approached 2,500 stores and an employee population of 30,000 we realized we had to deliver a consistent customer service message. We found that message in . . . **WAYMISH**. Needless to say we have a copy in every store, distribution center and office at Advance Auto Parts. In fact, we liked the book so much that we requested 2,000 copies with our company logo on the cover, as well as a chapter dedicated to our own customer service superstars."
—Advance Auto Parts

"**WAYMISH** packs a one-two punch: First, it evokes all the service frustrations you've ever experienced as a customer; Then, it dares you to examine your own business, to confront the **WAYMISH** within!"
—Warren Rubin, Chairman of the Workbench, New York NY

"I picked up your book this weekend. Even though I was finishing 2 other books I felt I had to read **WAYMISH** from start to finish! Since then I've glanced at it 100 times, a page here, a page there. With other training programs we don't seem to USE the information, but I can hear the **WAYMISH** warning with every customer I deal with! Way to go!"
—Heidi Keske, Training director of a major financial firm

"Your **WAYMISH** book is insightful and truly useful, no hogwash. It's about time customers were treated like actual people with actual minds and feelings. Bravo!"
—Reenie Feingold, President, Visual Horizons, Rochester NY

"**WAYMISH** is terrific. You have hit the nail on the head with this one! Not only is the concept brilliant (and obvious) but ties in with most people's personal experience. Employees hate to be wrong. I can visualize hundreds of sales trainers handing out thousands of copies of **WAYMISH** to front-line employees."
—Al Ries, Chairman, Ries & Ries, Focusing Consultants, Great Neck NY
Author of **Focus, Positioning, Marketing Warfare**

"**WAYMISH** uses documented, real life incidents—good and bad. Some illustrate a quick thinking, 'save the day' (and the customer) response. Others show mistreatment by insensitive, unthinking, procedure-driven employees. WAYMISH is a management wake-up call to empower our customer service contact employees to take care of the customer first!"
—Max Grassfield, President, Grassfield's Menswear, Denver CO

WHAT THIS BOOK IS — AND ISN'T

This is not a collection of stories about
stupid customer service mistakes.

And it's not yet another treatise on Customer Service Excellence.

It is a training book reported in storytelling style. .

1. Use these stories in brief staff and employee meetings.
    Be sure to have your *people* solve the problems.
    Have *them* volunteer answers and suggest better ways to
    serve customers.
2. In later company or departmental meetings, interject quick
    sessions on WAYMISH.
    Repeat examples and constant service suggestions will make
    your people aware how widespread the "Waymish bug" can
    be . . . and why no company is immune.
3. Over time these mini-lessons will reinforce in employees'
    minds how important Lifetime Customers can be to the
    success and continuation of your business.
4. For additional training materials or Customer Service
    seminars at your Company, contact us toll free at
    888-929-6474 (Waymish)

Ray Considine   *Ted Cohn*

"WAYMISH" means....

Botch
Bungle
Blunder
Bollix
Bugger Up

Fumble
Flounder
Wreck
Ruin . . .

Pick any word that will help you understand the disastrous effect that one minute's lousy service can have on a customer ready to buy . . . but mistreated, ready to leave you—forever

The worst words a business can hear from a customer are . . .
"I'll never come here again!"

Beware the WAYMISH. It's everywhere.

WAYMISH®

Why Are You Making It So Hard
for me to give you my money?

Ray Considine and Ted Cohn

WAYMISH® PUBLISHING COMPANY
PASADENA • CALIFORNIA

Book designed and type formatting by Bernard Schleifer
Cover designed by Alexander Swart, Swart Advertising

Manufactured in the United States of America

For more information, and quantity discounts please contact:

WAYMISH Publishing Company
#1125 Gateway Tower
3452 E. Foothill Boulevard
Pasadena, CA 91107

Call Toll Free: 1-888-WAYMISH
(1-888-929-6474)

Books can be inscribed and autographed in any quantity.
Ship within 48 hours if requested

Seventh Printing, 2005
ISBN 0-9673245-0-5

To my Inner Circle:
Christopher, for his expansive, "out-of-the box" ideas
Lisa, for her constancy, cheerfulness, closeness and advice
Isabel, who matures before your very eyes
Aislynn, a welcome, creative member of the family
And *Wayne,* who cares for the hectic harem in Oakland

RAY CONSIDINE

To Alice,
my love, who continues to open my eyes
to new ideas, vistas, and feelings.

TED COHN

CONTENTS

IMPORTANT NOTE:

All of these cases or stories are documented events reported to us by friends, business associates and several strangers who heard about our WAYMISH investigations.

Many, if not all the companies and organizations mentioned in this book are good, reputable firms. As you will see stated several times, the high level Mission Statement and goals of these firms are well defined.

The problems we've found demonstrated all too often are that the Corporate "Mission Message" does not penetrate through middle management or get down to what Jan Carlzon of SAS airlines calls "the Moments of Truth": Those crucial key moments when your front line is in personal contact with your customers.

The poor judgment and tragically frequent failures at this point of contact are what this book is about . . . along with some advice on How To Solve the problems and quash the WAYMISHes that are stealing your future profits.

WE HAD THE BOOK BUT NOT THE TITLE . . .

JOE BALLI IS AN executive with Muscolino Inventory Services of Arcadia, California. While you and I sleep, his brave souls sally forth to monstrous supermarkets and small retail stores and count . . . count items, SKUs (stock keeping units), check shelf tags, prices and such.

For accuracy these computer-carrying counters need to step up (literally) to see clearly what's on the top shelves. That requires small portable ladders.

So Joe Balli hikes himself off to one of those gigantic warehouse club stores to shop for one hundred (100) portable two-step ladders.

Entering the mammoth store, Joe approaches the first employee he sees and says, "I'd like to buy two-step ladders, a lot of them." "Aisle 8," the guy snaps. "Wa-wait a minute," Joe protests, "I mean I need a *hundred.*"

"Aisle 8," says the clerk over his shoulder and walks off. Disgusted, Joe goes in search of a manager. Finds him. Turns on his charm and says cheerily, "Say . . . I'd like to buy about 100 small step ladders." "Aisle 8," points the manager.

"No, No, No!" Joe protests, shaking his head side to side, "I mean I'd like to buy a **hundred** and maybe get some discount."

"We don't discount," snarls the manager.

Reaching out his hand in supplication Joe begs, "Listen! You order them from your base warehouse, bring 'em here on pallets and I'll get my truck to pick them up outside your building!" pointing through the doorway. "You don't even have to stock them!"

"We don't discount. Not interested," mutters the manager and starts walking off.

Totally frustrated Joe shouts, "**Why Are You Making It So Hard** . . . for me to give you my money??"

Ray heard the story from Joe, lifted the first letters of that priceless phrase and **W.A.Y.M.I.S.H.** was born. Thank you, Joseph.

Remember, this is a large store of a gigantic national chain. How will they ever know how much profit they lost from this one "original" Waymish?

So Beware-----------the Waymish can strike *anywhere*.

THE FACT IS . . .

THOUSANDS AND THOUSANDS of dollars in future business go down the drain daily in small and gigantic businesses . . . all because simple common sense treatment of customers hasn't penetrated down the full length of the Customer ladder—down to where the Customer is.

And in many cases, unfortunately, customer-defeating policies are created at the top rung of Management. Oh, the "new policy" may be great for Operations. Or give the company a better handle on Accounts Receivable. But the rules are too often barriers to buying, too often invisible to management but completely frustrating to customers trying to give your business their money.

These barriers are now called the "WAYMISHes." The thoughtless remark by a clerk. The rudeness just for a moment that infuriates the paying customer. Arrogance—the worst sin against customer service. A manager's indifference to a complaint. The refusal to stretch the rules just a bit to accommodate a customer with a special request.

All preventable. Most reversible. In almost every case described here the **lost customer could have been saved** . . . IF ONLY some alert employee, mid or higher manager had reacted fast enough to immediately "make it right" and rescue that temporarily infuriated, ready-to-quit customer.

Everybody who sells ANYthing should be fighting to
eliminate the worst words a customer can say:
"I'm never coming back here again!"

DOWN THE DRAIN

How to Lose $500, $5,000 & $50,000 customers in a flash!
And how the smallest attention can keep and nurture
a happy customer.

ONE CLIENT BLOWN AWAY

SMALL GRANDCHILD was arriving during the summer swimming season. Not yet old enough to navigate the pool depths, she could splash safely around in a rubber turtle, if properly inflated. Grandma doesn't "do" inflating. But since the regular pool service comes every Thursday, vacuums the pool briefly, checks the filter and departs 20 easy dollars richer, why not contact these folks and get a little extra service?

Grandma calls, explains arrival of granddaughter, asks if they have an inflatable turtle for sale, and what would it cost to blow it up and deliver it. The turtle is $9.95 and—ready?—to blow it up (apparently a major commercial undertaking) would cost $45.

(What??? Good-bye!)

Unbelievable. For one un-thinking WAYMISH moment, a piece-of-cake $1000-a-year pool-service account is gone with a refusal to put a puff of air into a rubber play toy. Not only that, how about the pool supplies, filter replacements and possible pump repairs. Stupido!

Well . . . our new pool man, Pedro, is quite nice. Very helpful. Maybe this summer we'll give him the "turtle test" . . .

Can You Help Me?

To every customer, **EVERY** associate/clerk/serving person regardless of title should be "my customer service representative." Don't you feel that way when you are trying to give a business your money?

As a customer, you don't need to be told, "Your server will be with you in a moment . . . " Or "You'll have to check at the front desk, I don't handle that here." Or our all-time favorite: "You've come to the wrong place." *Excuse me?* Aren't you employed here? Aren't you part of the staff of this business I am giving my money to? "Yes, but"— is the Classic non-solution reply (for which that person—or the manager—should be re-trained or fired). Your question as a customer is: *What about Solving my Problem???*

But things are improving

At Dayton-Hudson's TARGET discount stores (where you might not expect a lot of personal service) they have the Red Phones. Ahh! Can't find an item? Don't know a price? Confused about where to go in the store? Dial Operator.

Voice responds: "Operator . . ."

"Operator, I am near the toy department. I have an inflatable swimming pool lounge in a box. I tried your scanning machine at the end of the toy aisle, but it wouldn't scan the price."

"Just a moment please, I will get the toy buyer." (This is on a SUNDAY morning!)

Toy Buyer: "Ah—yes, sir. That is a clearance item. It's $4. If there is any problem at checkout, tell the checker Jose said it's $4. They can call me." Take box. Go through checkout. Relay Jose's message. Checker smiles, "Four dollars and 31 cents with tax. Thank you. Next?"

LESSON: This store knows how to . . . Answer the question. Solve the problem. Get the money. Move on.

And . . .

At some Marriotts, the doorman can now take your baggage, assign you a room, check you in, get you a rental car. Yippee!

Maybe, just maybe, we are moving closer to the Total Service concept where any employee asked by any guest will give the one and only profit-making, customer-for-life reply:

I CAN HANDLE THAT FOR YOU.

The Right Way

To experience this feeling of "all around, take-care-of-it-now" service, try a Ritz Carlton Hotel. You aren't *pointed* in a direction. You are *escorted* there. Ritz people come from behind desks (a miracle!), leave their lobby posts (wow!) and walk with you to the Vienna Room or whatever your destination—regardless of distance.

[How does your company handle its "direction" requests?]

To ensure this commitment requires that EVERY ONE of your staff and employees "buys into" this pledge of "all around" service. It takes Training and Repetition and an insistence your employees understand Rule Number One:
   When you see, hear or meet a customer, all other duties and activities are put on Hold.
First, foremost and fanatically . . . SERVE THE CUSTOMER.

THE GASOLINE WARS

Gary Hall has a nice mid-sized printing company in Pasadena, California. Gary is an even-tempered guy. He doesn't make waves. Produces quality, on-time printing. Is gracious and is inclined to compromise rather than argue. Excellent at keeping his customers.

Gary has delivery trucks—plural—for his print shop. For a long time he's been patronizing the nearest gas station—right across the street from his recently expanded plant. Suddenly that company announces they are dropping gasoline credit cards, all credit cards and turning to a strictly cash basis. OK for them (and it worked for the company's share of market) but a pain for Gary.

Now he needs to get cash daily for the drivers. Cash advances mean complications, more bookkeeping. So Gary suggests to the station: "Let's set up a running account." He would pay monthly. After all he's been dealing with this across-the-street station for a long time. Make sense?

Not to this station manager. His answer is NO. N-O. Brilliant, huh? Especially when you "do the lifetime value numbers": Gary's trucks use $700-$800 worth of gas a month. Even without a calculator that's approaching $10,000 a year.

And for that decision, the man right across the street (if he's watching) sees Gary's trucks drive in and out and out and in of—his competitor's station just up the street. As pal Murray Raphel in his *Direct Marketing* columns asks: **"Why do they do that?"**

We don't have the answer. Or any sympathy.

THE CARE PACKAGE

Jim Smith's company had been banking with Barnett Banks in Florida for years. As the company's deposits grew, Barnett management paid absolutely no attention to the account. No one called. No one visited. No one cared.

Recently, Jim went to the local Barnett branch office with an assistant to arrange for a large wire transfer. Three bank officers were busy with people at their desks. A fourth manager was on the phone, apparently enjoying a personal call.

Irritated, Jim placed himself right in front of the manager who finally took notice of him, cupped his hand over the mouthpiece, and sternly ordered Jim to "sign in." Jim: "I'm not signing IN anywhere. I'm signing OUT the $1.8 million we have on deposit."

Pandemonium among the four bank officers.

Too late. A new bank has treated Jim with care and respect. Later, a letter came from Barnett, asking for another chance. No one called. No one visited. No one cared.

NOT ONE BITE!

Joan Pajunen, a consultant in Toronto, was shopping for cocktail party items at a grocery store where she'd spent about $400 a month for ten years.

While waiting, Joan spied a display of candy in an open box on the shelf, surrendered to temptation, reached over and took a piece of candy.

The manager saw her, stormed over, chastised her in front of what felt like a thousand other customers and *took back* the $70 worth of items she'd already placed in her cart!

Quiz: What were the manager's worst WAYMISHes?
1. He didn't know a ten-year customer by sight.
2. He failed to weigh a single piece of candy against a $70 order.
3. He demeaned a customer in public. [Never, never done!]
4. The store lost not only the sale, and a ten-year, $40,000+ Customer, but countless other customers as Joan repeated the insulting story around town.

[A super-expensive WAYMISH committed.]

But . . . other than those few missteps, that manager was really alert for candy nappers, huh?

BUDGET GETS CUT

Dale Byrne, bright, energetic, impatient founder/pusher of INTACTIX, won't (repeat won't) waste time, even half a minute. Things gotta happen or he's on your case!

A covey of us flew into Denver together, were bussed to the slightly remote base of Budget Rent a Car. Dale speaks: "Why are we here? Is this Hertz?" (Well . . . not exactly.) Dale's upset but says, "Let's make the most of it."

We load the considerable conference baggage into the rental trunk. Dale assumes the driver's seat and spurts for the exit. A hefty, very relaxed, slow moving "cop" is at the gate to check rental papers, walk the vehicle for dings and dents and then open the exit gate.

PROBLEM: There is a car ahead of us and our portly gate cop hasn't heard the word Hurry. He meanders around examining the car in front of us. Mr. Byrne is about to go around the blocking car and make a Steve McQueen getaway. Budget Cop gives us one glance and continues to chat nonchalantly with the driver of the car ahead.

As Dale edges up to the rear bumper of the exiting car, he calmly but forcibly asks Cop Man, "Why so slow? Can't renters get out without all this folderol?"—and then says, "Maybe we should have gone to Hertz."

"Then why dontcha?" was Budget Man's reply with a wide smile. And then begins his s-l-o-w inspection of our car. Dale's retort as he snatched the rental papers out of Cop Man's hands: "Don't worry, we will never rent from you again." Cop could care less. Gives us a derisive "gotcha!" smile and waves a casual good-bye as we zoom out the gate.

It's good-bye for Budget. Cop Man may not care but Prez Byrne is tough, means what he says. Budget is forever out of the INTACTIX travel budgets.

The top brass of Budget are undoubtedly competent. They are into Customer Service, of course. And the corporate mandate most surely is some version of "Take Care of the Customer." Yet one dummy at the Moment of Truth—in contact with the customer— blows thousands of dollars in future business . . . by being arrogant.

Arrogance is the cardinal sin of service.

NUMBER PLEASE . . .

Prospect calls a company.

The executive that the customer is calling does not answer.

Operator comes on the line.

"Could you take a message, please, for Mr. Richland and tell him that the reports—"

"Sir! I'm not used to taking such long messages." (Is this Lily Tomlin in a TV skit?)

Customer: "This message isn't that long."

Lily: "Sir! If you'd see what small pads we have here at the switch-board you'd understand." (It MUST be Lily Tomlin!)

She continues: "Ya know, we have three businesses and five phone numbers . . . "

Customer surrendering: "OK! Do you have a number where I can reach him?"

"No."

And she hangs up.

Have you checked your company's telephone manners lately?

Are you sure your incoming calls are being handled competently?

Or maybe you've resorted to money-saving, automated voice mail answering.

May we suggest one thing? Survey your largest paying clients to see what they think of your automated, cost-saving voice mail system? Surprises could be in store.

You may want to investigate some creative special by-pass code for your most profitable callers. Such codes do exist. They also make the special customers feel special

The purpose of business . . .

If we define **service** as **mutually satisfying relationships** between an organization and its customers, how far removed from this definition of orientation, training, and customer service is the way most of us spend our day?

We introduce a supermarket cashier to her job by showing her how to scan, how to handle change, checks, credit cards, returns and other necessary basic routines. We teach a new salesperson about the products, prices, terms, forms to fill out, commission and expense routines.

Managers spend their time on the phone, writing and reading memos and reports, dealing with personnel and customer problems, going to meetings and occasionally thinking and planning.

All of these activities are necessary. But if we are concerned with extraordinary service, we have to put them in the context of the primary purpose of every employee, at every level—*to create and maintain positive customer relationships.*

Peter Drucker said it fifty years ago—

the purpose of BUSINESS is to create a customer.

What's the message?

Start your orientation, training and performance measurements *not* with activities but with customer relationships.

With this approach of creating customer relationships as your base, the activities fall into their proper place—as TOOLS, not ends in themselves. Include measures of customer satisfaction and retention (where applicable) in your performance standards.

Teach people to smile, be cordial, when dealing with customers before you teach them to scan.

Teach people to listen and acknowledge the feelings of others before they become product experts. Feelings come first.

Teach people to ask questions before they give advice.

Investigate how an employee who is working on a report, straightening inventory, counting cash, or handling a personnel matter treats an encounter with a customer? If the answer is: the customer is interrupting the REAL work or is a distraction from the REAL job—prepare for the invasion of the WAYMISH!

And to improve the probability that your training will be used by the right people, spend a lot of time hiring people who feel comfortable with a service attitude.

Better for Both Sides

A WAYMISH almost inevitably creates frustration or unpleasantness for everyone involved—the customer and the employee. So institutionalizing an anti-WAYMISH philosophy and an empowered process to avoid a majority of these aggravating incidents will provide the "grease" needed to ease the friction in these upsetting situations.

Reducing or eliminating WAYMISHes will obviously enhance your profit and strengthen your customer relationships. It will also produce a non-economic benefit that is a psychological dividend: fewer WAYMISHes will result in fewer cases of the sandpaper rubbings that occur when people react in their internal, as well as customer relationships.

So, eliminating WAYMISHes is not only good for the profit, it's good for the psyche!

LET ME HEAR THOSE COMPLAINTS

The harder you listen, the easier to keep the customer!

THE PENTIUM CHIP incident is a case. The computer chip was faulty. Intel, the manufacturer of the chip, insisted that the customers complaining about the faulty chip had to prove they had not performed any complex mathematical functions that might have been miscalculated! WAYMISH?

Dell, a Pentium user, on the other end of the customer service spectrum, called all its Pentium customers and offered to replace the chip at no charge if there was a problem. Immediately.

Dell reportedly called 400,000 customers to gauge customer satisfaction. Know what they foundl? Fifteen percent of the accounts called wanted to buy *more Dell products!*

[How often are you contacting your customers on a
random sampling basis?]

WE WANT YOU BACK!

The restaurant chain is called McCormick and Schmick's. Funny name. (Reminds you of that great ad slogan: "With a name like Smuckers, it has to be good.") McSchmick's is good.

STORY: A finnick (a picky, precise, super-neat type person) decided to sit on the outside patio rather than inside McSchmick's.

Our impatient, foot-tapping finnick wants his drink Right Now

. . . if you please! The problem is classic—busy, popular restaurant, rush hour at lunch, his is the only table occupied on the patio. Out of sight, slightly out of mind, so they didn't spot him for a few minutes. This does not suit the man.

He is eventually served—with apologies—but then there is another w-a-i-t for lunch to be served at his outside location. As he leaves fuming, he declares to his companion the infamous "This is it!" message, "I am never coming here again!" A large spender lost?

Not quite.

There are people locally who are so fond of McSchmick's that when they hear his complaint, next time at the restaurant, they tell the ebullient hostess, "You might have lost a good customer" and name him.

"Oh no!" comes the cry of pain from Andrea, the manager. "Please . . . give us his name and let us contact him." And they do.

The letter to Mr. Finnick from McCormick and Schmick's says, "We know you feel you were mistreated but give us another chance" and offers a $50 gift certificate for dining. Wow!

Now all he has to do is book the reservation and see what else these heads-up, taking-care-of-business McSchmick's people will do to . . . KEEP THAT CUSTOMER!

Are you rewarding everyone who "tips you off" to a lost customer?

How Suite It Is!

Ritz Carlton Hotel, Washington DC. The TV set could not be seen from the bed, the toilet made an annoying noise which did not stop. Reported at midnight, the concierge apologized no one was available at the moment to fix the problems.

Next day, management moved the guest to a suite accompanied with champagne, fruit, cheese, and a *handwritten* letter of apology from the general manager.

TCOB = Takin' Care Of Business.

Thus multiplying the legend of the Ritz.

I REALLY DON'T KNOW HOW THIS HAPPENED, SIR . . .

I hate that phrase, don't you?

On a holiday weekend, a guest hunkered down at the Ojai Inn. Gorgeous California golf resort. By leaving word on the message machine, guest invited Wade Cannon, a Santa Barbara compadre, to drive the 38 miles for a leisurely lavish Sunday brunch the next morning.

Ojai guest awoke Sunday morning. Waited for Wade's call. Repeatedly called front desk for messages. No message? Strange. Wade is ex-Navy. Always on time. Still uses ETAs (Estimated Time of Arrival) and other snappy nautical phrases. Routinely arrives for departing planes an hour ahead of time, etc.

Hunger set in. Guest gave up, had buffet brunch. Still no Wade. Called Wade. Got his Answering Service. The frustrated voice mail message angrily said; "I left three messages for you! Where are you?" And a final message: "This is the fourth and final message, amigo! Thanks a lot. Wasted my entire holiday morning riding 76 miles down there and back. You weren't even registered!"

Guest (Considine) rushed to the front desk and demanded they check their records.

"Sorry sir—you are not registered."

"I'm WHAT? NOT registered???"

"I really don't know how this happened, sir . . . " (Now, there's a customer-killer phrase).

Result: Guest goes ballistic. "Check your records, man! I spent the night here for $195 in room 176!"

"Are you Mr. Raymond?"

"I am Raymond **Considine.**"

Sunday morning clerk casually, "Oh sir, we have you registered as Mr. *Raymond*." (Smile of sympathy as though I am the idiot.) "That's probably why we couldn't take your friend's message." (Another smirk.)

I took a stroll on the lawn in preference to committing murder in public. My heart rate was settling down to normal. I was paged. Paged?

Wade had arrived? No, the Manager had somehow heard of my problem. Good for him. First, he insisted on comping the $195 room. Moderately mollified, I mumbled a suggestion I pay for the brunch—since I ate it. He said, "No, absolutely not." Then, salesman that he was, he asked, "What do you do?" Hearing I am a professional speaker, he gently suggested he show me his auditorium and meeting facilities. After a $195 comp, plus a magnificent brunch, how could I refuse?

Reminded me of a lesson my old Boston Boss Leonard Raymond taught me: A really good salesman is one who . . . after he gets into trouble with the customer, thinks smart, comes up with an answer and then re-sells the customer with an **irresistible offer**.

Leonard was correct. This guy did comp me for a fairly high tab. I felt better. The Manager's investment in righting a WAYMISH on the spot paid off. I was happy. Wade wasn't. That was my problem.

And yes, I'd recommend Ojai . . . and over the last couple of years, I have. And will. That manager preferred what Feargal Quinn of Dublin, Ireland calls the "Boomerang Principle"—he brought me back—and resold me on his hotel—as a customer and as an advocate by reacting immediately.

Ask and You Shall Receive

A managing partner of a CPA firm was thinking customer service. He called the 25 largest clients and asked for three minutes of the CEO's time to answer two questions:

THE SURVEY:
What do you *like* about our firm's service?
What do you *not* like about our firm . . . or any other CPA?

[NOTE: This is the best and simplest survey any business will ever need.]

Three annoyances that surfaced in the "didn't like" question turned into a gold mine for the firm: (1) Top clients didn't understand the invoices; (2) Resented annual fee increases; and (3) Were annoyed by personnel turnover assigned to their accounts.

Here is simple intelligence applied: (1) The firm immediately started sending detailed invoices and urged and invited clients to ask questions. (If clients didn't trust the billing, how could they trust the professional's recommendations?); (2) The firm instituted a campaign to CUT fees by having partners do less of the routine tasks, turning that work over to their clients' internal accounting staffs; and (3) followed through by promising that one staff member would be assigned to the account for at least three years.

The payoff for these three-minute, two-question calls?

The next year, the firm had a considerable jump in new clients by referral and *recommendation*.

There's the phone. You know who your top clients are. The two "like" and "don't like" questions are above. . . .

BY THE SEAT OF HIS PANTS

Ray was visiting Murray Raphel's clothing store in Atlantic City a few years back and kibitzing with Murray who—as always—was keeping an eagle eye on what was happening on the sales floor.

Suddenly, a man burst through the front door brandishing a pair of trousers and shouting, "These pants are no good! I spent my money and I—"

Murray vaulted out of his chair and was out on the floor in a flash like a fireman answering a four-alarm fire.

"**SIR!**" Murray shouted loudly enough to override the angry customer's voice, "Sir . . ." crooned Murray, a little softer the second time, "Please do not shout in my store. If there is a problem with these (seizing the trousers and tossing them carelessly into a corner), I will (counting off on his fingers)—One, give you a new pair of pants. Two, fix the ones you have. Three, give you the cash to go to another tailor. Four, give you your money back. Now, (long pause—very effective). . . *Just tell me what you want.*"

As an observer to the scene, Ray smiled, took out a pen and wrote something down. Later, Murray, with wrinkled brow said, "What was so funny?"

Ray said (and meant it): "Man, you just created a legendary phrase for me—*"Just tell me what you want"*. . . . That customer wouldn't ask for your wife, half the store, or a lien on your house . . . he just wants a decent pair of pants."

Murray smiled, nodded in agreement. "Good . . . good," he muttered—and of course stored that phrase away in his mind to write in his columns, newsletters and promotions. After all . . . Murray is one of the original Great Brain Robbers.

It Works

[Considine] I have used that phrase—"Just tell me what you want" hundreds of times in speeches and seminars. True . . . managers balk at first, afraid to allow their people to say to a customer, "Just tell me what you want." The manager is afraid he'll have to "give the store away."

Then I remind them of Nordstrom Department Stores where their fabled service never "draws the line." There is no limit to satisfying the customer. Witness the one legend of a customer returning an automobile tire—which the customer insisted he had bought at Nordstrom. But they don't carry tires. Yet Nordstrom credited the customer's account.

How many times has THAT mythical story been told? Would your Company pay $40 for a legend of service like this—and a hundred more "Nordstrom tales of incredible service?"

Think about it. Is advertising and blowing your own horn in media really the best way to attract customers?

Or is the better way to create legendary service by Taking Care of every service problem by ruling in favor of the customer?

THE BILLION DOLLAR POST-IT

Viking Office Supplies is a huge international paper products company. Their competition? Staples, Office Max, Office Depot and independent locally owned stationery stores.

Fascinating thing about Irwin Helford's Viking company: it has better service than any other stationer. You don't have to move—except to pick up the phone, order today, get it tomorrow. Order it early enough in the morning, you may get the delivery in the afternoon! And they are not next door or just down the block.

How does Irwin remind you to "stick with Viking?" He sends a catalog EVERY WEEK. And . . . it has the name of your current secretary or buyer printed on the cover! (Names change when secretary changes because the new lady wants HER name on the weekly Viking mail.)

So our secretary ordered padded mailbags (the better to ship you your Waymishes), paper clips, pens, highlighters, Post-Its, whatever. Next day—everything is delivered. Problem: the Post-Its were the microscopic postage stamp size. Owner hates these miniatures! No room to write. So secretary called Viking's 800 number, asked if next time we could trade the too-small Post-Its for larger medium-size ones. Next day (Note—no order was placed), Viking man arrived with a packet of medium-size Post-Its and when she attempted to return the micros, Viking Man smiled and said, "Just keep 'em. You can find a use for them" and departed.

Questions: Excellent PR? Definitely. Or, cynically, is it cheaper for Viking to donate a pittance of small Post-Its rather than to pick them up, re-enter them into the system. . . .

Doesn't matter. Who do you think the secretary calls when we need any paper products, laser printer toner, or . . .?

The Harvard Business School gurus call this customer-linked attention, the Learning Relationship. We know you; we remember you; we'll take care of you. Viking has already learned that lesson.

It's Always Our Fault

Irwin Field's father-in-law, Ike, was in a business that processed soybeans into soybean oil and meal. The meal was packed in 100-pound sacks that were stacked in rail cars for shipment to customers. Twelve percent water content was the acceptable trade practice.

Irwin learned the business by sharing an office with Ike and by picking up the phone whenever he got a "thumbs up" signal from Ike. Learning by listening in. One day a good customer called, Irwin got the signal and heard the following:

Customer: "Ike, we got a problem. Your guys must have turned on the faucet a little too long. We have bags of soymeal floating in water." (What probably happened was that the bags were piled too high in the freight car and the extra weight of the top bags had squeezed water into the bottom bags.)

"Don't say another word!" interrupted Ike. "Whatever happened, *it's our fault.* Here's what I want you to do: pull out and destroy any bags you think have too much water. Then figure out how many bags are no good, how much the labor cost was to pull and get rid of the bags. Also add the cost of your office people who keep track of labor costs. Send me a slip of paper with the total amount and I'll send you a check the day I get it."

Imagine the amazement of that customer! And his reaction? The amount he sent in was no more than half the actual cost of sorting out the bad bags. And how would you describe the future relationship of Irwin's father-in-law's business and this customer? Solid.

Years pass. Now Irwin's son joins the business. The first business lesson he was taught was the "Ike story": Whenever there is a problem . . . *it's always our fault.* A message worth passing down through the generations—lose the profit, lose the sale, but Keep the Customer.

SYNDICATING THE ANSWER
People, Productivity, and Procedures

First, Define the Problem

ONE OF Considine's problem-solving methods in his management speeches is "Syndicating Solutions": If a problem happens once, it could be just an accident, an aberration. A one time thing. Solution: Solve it, please.

The second time it occurs, alert management says, "Hey? Again? How come?"

Message: Attention, People . . . we have a possible problem here.

The third time is the signal to *syndicate a solution*: "OK. Looks like we have a recurring problem. Next time it happens, here's what we do." The goal of the syndicating theory is to get agreement on the solution, so the next time the work flow doesn't stop, time isn't wasted—again—to figure out what to do.

The procedure is laid down and the answer is now automatic . . . and works . . . IF. But there is one IF.

"Syndicating answers works," Considine says, "only IF you have a 'Freedom of Speech' atmosphere in your Company." That means a confidence so your people can talk about ANY problem without "looking dumb" and without being criticized.

In a nutshell—you welcome problems.
You don't beat up people who make a mistake.

Unless of course you are perfect and have never made a mistake yourself.

Another, more basic way to handle a recurring problem is to look for the root cause: what system, policy or procedure is not working and how do we fix it for good?

It's a Matter of Trust

Having your people trust you enough as a manager (at any level) so they can constantly report problems to you—small, large, strange, suspect—is the ideal channel to eliminate the inevitable mistakes in business.

When people can report their own failures without fear, recrimination, demotion or dismissal, Management will be able to (a) see the signals of impending trouble, (b) sense recurring patterns of possible major problems . . . and (c) sniff out a future WAYMISH before it bites you in the profits.

Making it Right

ChemLawn is a company that has an interesting selling sequence, planned for the key purpose: *to keep the customer.*

First, they hire personable, attractive, "Mr. Clean" types and dress them in white jump suits with green trim. Next, when expanding territories they form a caravan of five or six of their squeaky clean white and green trucks on a weekend and quietly drive single file 'round and 'round through the new prospect neighborhood creating a presence and identification. The following week the men in white make their opening sales calls.

They work by appointment, and legend has it, they are there promptly at the appointed time. (Impressive to the housewife accustomed to the utility announcements: "Service some time between 8 AM and 4 PM.")

Each soil treatment is accompanied with a note on a small white and green sign planted in your lawn. The message is professional instruction: "Water every 2 days." "Do not water for 2 days." After each visit a note is left on your door. Most handy for those householders not at home during lawn-curing times.

Unhappy with results? Greenery not growing? Call ChemLawn and they are there in a flash. The plant spray treatment turn your lawn sorta brown? They re-sod, by god! That is a $50 to $60 retail investment—in the customer.

Which leads to this strong advice: Lose a profit. Lose a sale. NEVER LOSE A CUSTOMER! (In California, we are going on our tenth year with the men in white and green. It seems there is just no problem they cannot solve or make right.)

For Management: Complaints

Sharon Hanes Brown, a service/sales consultant, summarized the reasons for organizing complaint procedures in an article in a Construction Equipment Distribution publication.

First, the reasons to have a systemized complaint program:

A. The complainer is your Customer. You have a relationship which, when tested by a complaint, is a positive base from which to reestablish your concern.

B. The complaint signals that the customer wants help, a much stronger basis to deal with than the customer who "melts away"—moves, disappears.

The company can now join with the customer in solving the problem—(and eliminating the WAYMISH)—by forming a *partnership* which not only shows you care, but puts the company in a better position to manage the situation.

C. Complaints are the source of new ideas in every part of your business. But—be prepared to listen and **not fight back**. Of course, customers can be unreasonable by asking for things they want but you cannot or don't want to provide. But they also can be the needle that hypes you to challenge what you're now doing and ask ,"Are we doing enough?"

Here's how to institutionalize complaints and make them part of your continuous-learning organization.

1. **Write them down.** Today that means computerize them in a system that will give you sensible, useable feedback. From that, develop trends that point to the need for study and action.

2. **Investigate all closed accounts.** Why did they leave? What did we do wrong? What can we do to get them back? Do we need to make a special offer to get them back? (Case: Customer switched long-distance phone carriers. A few days later, the losing company called and asked "would you come back?"—but didn't ask why the switch had been made or what they could have done—or could do now—to keep the account. A totally wasted follow-up, like so many poorly planned marketing efforts.)

3. **Set performance measures for handling complaints.** Let every one of your people involved in the complaint system know what is expected. Clarify accountability, and build an effective complaint record database.

4. **Use complaints to develop new services.** And drop those services or products that cause more problems than they're worth. Don't forget to inform the customers who were using those dropped services and make them an offer to stay!

5. **Be Proactive.** Don't wait for complaints. Invite them! Use an 800 toll-free number. Procter & Gamble does; GE does; Whirlpool does; the catalog companies do. Ask for any problems in your ordering and shipping telephone calls; provide postage-paid reply forms with mailed statements or invoices. Make it easy for customers to respond. Let them tell you if there are WAYMISHes you haven't discovered yet.

6. **Follow-up on the complaint handling procedure.** How can you make sure the customer was as satisfied as you could make him or her? Now use that follow-up as a means of soliciting additional information. (Remember, Dell computers phoned their customers to solve the Pentium chip problem and 15 percent of the calls resulted in *additional business*.)

Another Approach:
Learning from Competition

THE PLAN: Have ten customer-contact employees spend up to half an hour (on company time) each week—in two different competitors' stores, warehouses or offices:

(1) ordering or returning an item
(2) getting a quote or handling a complaint
(3) have them report back
    (a) where are competitors doing better, or worse
    (b) how can you exploit the weaknesses
    (c) what are none of the competitors doing that **we should be** doing.

This idea will cost you $6000 a year. $12 an hour times ten people a week equals $120 a week, times 50 weeks. It equals the cost (or loss) of one customer who spends a $120 a week with you. Cheap.

Employees feel they're an important part of the team, they become sensitive to competitors. Helps them challenge what you're doing. Stimulates ideas. Probably exposes your people to some WAYMISHes of competitors. Seeing the problems in other stores makes them believers. Demonstrates that anti-WAYMISH consciousness and actions are a vital part of their job. Be sure to have them report their findings to your other customer contact people before the next team goes out shopping competitors.

Yet Another Approach:
Study Your Service From All Angles

Karl Otto Skogland was Managing Director of the SAS Hotel in Denmark near the Copenhagen airport. Many of his check-outs were rushing to the airport.

Karl is a sharp, observant manager and an active believer in MBWA: Managing By Walking Around. One morning Karl was standing in the lobby watching the early morning exodus of guests when an idea hit him. Why are there only the regular number of cashiers working when *everyone* in the lobby is checking out?

Anxious to try his idea (called Ready-Fire-Aim) immediately, that afternoon as guests were checking IN, he reversed the procedure and opened all the spaces at the Reception and Cashier counters for check-INs. It worked wonderfully. He got compliments.

How could he keep pushing his idea out further? "Ah! Look!" he said the next morning. Here were exiting guests in line balancing styrofoam cups of coffee and juggling baggage as they waited to check out. The main hotel dining room is quite close to the check-out counter but is closed in the morning since a top-floor skyroom is the featured full-service breakfast place.

Karl Otto proceeded to open the closest section of the lobby dining room across from the front desk for orange juice, coffee and Copenhagen "danish"—FREE—for guests in a rush to make planes. (By the way, in SAS Hotels, you can check your baggage for the flight at the porter's desk near the front door and have it delivered directly to your flight.)

Have You Tried CAD-CAM Lately?

Have you "stepped back" lately and looked at your business from a totally different point of view: *how your customers would like to do business with you?*

Considine calls this the CAD-CAM concept (from Computer Assisted Design, the computer manipulating technique architects, car companies and design studios use. It means turning your business upside down, sideways, rear view, top view. Viewing your business from an entirely NEW vantage point.

If you're looking for a novel, brain-stimulating meeting idea, try this CAD-CAM concept with your associates and totally challenge the way you are doing business now.

Three Easy Pieces

James E. Robinson, III, former CEO of American Express, set these goals for his company:
- Define service from the customer's point of view
- Measure service delivery with the same objectivity and precision that is used to measure productivity, costs and revenues
- Involve all employees at every level in the quality service process

Robinson's three areas are simple but hard to do. Find out everything your customers want; build systems, procedures, decision-making points and the measuring tools to check how they're functioning; and finally, in our biased point of view, recognize and reward your people who deliver the service.

Four Quick Ways to Wipe Out WAYMISHes

- Have your employees work in the customer end of the business for a week.
- Have employees visit a competitor and ask each of them to report on one thing "they do better than we do."
- Encourage employees to go through your whole process—from the phone inquiry, to a sale, merchandise returns, complaints and a credit check.
- Evaluate all policies once every three years. Personnel and customer policies should be reviewed annually.

COMMUNICATION

The Right Hand Often Knoweth Not What
the Left Hand Doeth . . .
and some suggested solutions.

I N 25 PLUS YEARS of doing management seminars and asking participants at every level to "List the five most troublesome problems in your business," we found the Number One problem ALWAYS comes out—Communication.

What that word means to the people in those audiences is a fascinating exercise that brings out the most basic problems of any company: It's people trying to "know what's going on."

Here's an example . . .

"NETMA" *[Nobody Ever Tells Me Anything!]*

The original story was that the newly appointed president of a major airline put a small pin on his lapel that spelled NETMA. Then he began his tour of the major airports. His purpose? To see how his employees were handling customer service.

Arriving in a large city about noon, and as yet unknown to the company employees, he stood in a fairly long line like a customer at his airline's counter.

Seeing that the one female counter agent was swamped, he stepped forward and said, "Miss, I'm with the airline, how can I help?" She snapped, "Put these destination tags on those bags as I hand them to you and it's gotta be quick."

The president had no experience with tagging bags but being a bright guy caught on quickly. When the crowd thinned, he smiled at her and introduced himself. She was stunned and when he asked, "Where are our other people during this noon rush hour?" She shrugged with embarrassment and said, "I don't know. *Nobody ever tells me anything.*"

The president pointed to his NETMA lapel pin and said, "Well, that's my job and I think I see where we can start with this business of Communication!"

Have you reviewed your NETMA factor lately?

KNOW THY PRODUCT

Xerox advertised a new word processor.

Interested buyer calls the advertised 800 number. . . . Has three questions: what is the size of the machine, what is its storage capacity, and how much does it cost?

The person answering knew none of the answers, transferred the call to another Xerox person who gave the answers to the first two questions but said he couldn't tell the price.

"Only dealers could quote a price." But, he would be happy to provide dealer phone numbers.

Without some idea of the price the would-be buyer was not inclined to make another call. Sarcastically, he asked the Xerox person if the price was between $1 and $5,000. No response.

RESULT: One lost sale from an interested, serious buyer. After paying to advertise the product, why was Xerox making it so hard for him to spend his money with their company?

Copy This:

We all know that Xerox is an excellent company. So why are we picking on them?

Only to make the point that in spite of lofty corporate Mission Statements and enviable service commitments, much too often "the word" does not get down through that thicket of management layers to the point-of-customer contact training.

Why would Xerox NOT allow their people contacting the public (read "buyers with money") to know or disclose the answers to easily predictable questions like . . . Size, Storage and Price of a *New* Product?

Do the Xerox promotional people who created the ad and published the 800 number to draw response have any control over distributing basic Product Information to the field and phone people who handle the responses?

Or is this the classic corporate cop-out: "Oh, that's a different division."

"TWO DIFFERENT COMPANIES"

As active business consultants, we have both encountered this "not my problem—not our division" syndrome. Just look at the examples here: Budget, Avis, Xerox, Amex and on and on. Of course every company will say, "Oh yes, we all work together. We have to. It's One Company." Yet we find the WAYMISH inserting itself in between the layers of good intentions and corporate statements.

FOR EXAMPLE: In Foster & Kleiser, a large Los Angeles based outdoor billboard company, the sign-painting-manufacturing "backroom" felt strongly that the "frontroom" sales guys were a bunch of martini-swigging wise guys who made all the money while "us sign makers did all the work."

The result was that billboard posting promises made by Sales were taken rather lightly by the Sign Making crews. Consequence: Customer Service was ragged, future business was in jeopardy, large ad agencies were unhappy. So Boss Ross Barrett and VP Charlie Hardison took the two factions off to a distant location and thrashed it out.

The message was—WE ARE ALL ONE COMPANY.

PASSING THE PROBLEM DOWN— DOESN'T WORK

A triple division problem was evident with Bendix Mobile Homes of Canada. The manufacturing plants pushing for production quotas were not quite finishing every detail.

A roof awry here, a seam ever so slightly open there, workmanship approaching shoddy but—"get those units out of here and get them to the distributor yards!"

And so it went: the distributors would shrug and say, "Hey—not our problem. Manufacturing sent them this way. All we do is move them on to the Sales locations."

Then the local Bendix selling team would be on the verge of a sale when some sharp-eyed buyer would begin to spot a crack here and a small problem there and what? Lost sale. It was the hey day of mobile home sales in Canada and the customer had options (competitors plural) within walking distance.

LISTEN, LEARN, DECIDE
and admit you don't have all the answers

The solution was across-Canada meetings at all plants with the theme: "There's Got To Be A Better Way!" The final session, with 86 key management personnel at one huge open square table, was called "Wagon Train." ALL complaints, gripes, bitches and recommendations were welcomed. Corporate management was *not* allowed to debate or defend any of the division criticisms. They were instructed "just to listen"—very difficult for in-charge-type executives. And, except for a few "hiccups" of automatic interruption (followed by quick apologies), a huge array of large and small grievances was aired, shared, and solved to a gratifying degree.

NOTE: The best of all techniques was this: (1) Management seriously listened; (2) Management considered what had transpired in a private session; (3) The next morning management produced three easels. One had a large YES; a second, an equally large NO; and the third had a bold question mark on it.

The moderator then revealed the pages under the YES/NO/? covers. "Here are the ones we will correct—YES . . . Here are the ones we cannot—NO . . . and why we cannot, at this time. And finally, these with the question mark baffle us. We don't know what to do with these!"

The utter can-do attitude and overnight decision-making went further to solidify that company, more than anything the moderator had seen in many moons of consulting.

These instances could be called SUPER WAYMISHes because they are company-generated, company-condoned in trying to "make quotas"—in manufacturing units shipped, distributor units shipped, and sales units sold. And yet, overall Company goals are endangered because individual attitudes and turf protection are defeating the Company as a profit-making enterprise.

We understand Jack Welch, legendary leader of GE, was one of the first to act on the destructiveness of this syndrome and established his "tell it like it is" Management Center that meets monthly at Croton-on-Hudson to combat just such problems.

WE ARE ALL ONE COMPANY.
Are you?

When was this organization memo published and by whom?

"We trained hard, but it seemed every time we were beginning to form into teams, we would be reorganized . . . We tend to meet any new situation by reorganizing; and a wonderful method it can be for creating the illusion of progress while producing confusion, inefficiency, and demoralization of our subordinates."

PETRONIUS ARBITER, Grecian Navy 210 BC

Back to Top-Level Management Goals. . .

As mentioned, we have great respect for Xerox and the other companies mentioned in these WAYMISH exceptions. Let's look at the Xerox charter.

Xerox's strategy has five points:

1. Total commitment of senior management
2. Quantifiable standards and measurements
3. Education and training
4. Recognition and rewards
5. Effective and consistent communication

This strategy is based on a few basic assumptions:

1. Management doesn't have all the answers.
2. All people have ideas about how their jobs can be done more effectively.
3. People closest to the problems often have the best solutions (although that didn't work in the previous example about Bendix Mobile Home).

 All excellent companies realize there is a tremendous source of knowledge and creativity that can be tapped through employee involvement. [Study or re-examine the lessons of W. Edwards Deming who, after being refused by U.S. industry at the end of World War II, took his quality and employee involvement concepts to Japan—and you know the rest of that story.]

LET'S TALK EMPLOYEES . . .

There are three levels of employees—A, B & C.

"A's" are the few exceptional super performers. They require only three basic "strokes"—R. A. R.—Recognition, Appreciation and Reward. These few A's are naturally motivated. They want to do a good job.

 Treat them correctly. Respect their abilities. Be aware of their concern for your company and be sure someone in authority hears their recommendations of how to make your company better. They know those answers. Listen to them. Enroll them as your unofficial advisors.

"**Bs**" are the worker Bees: numerous, willing, mainstays in any business. The backbone. They make it run. With proper attention they can be taught add-on sales techniques by creating and insisting on each employee delivering a "Selling Sentence."

The universal proof of this is McDonald's. They hire ordinary people and give them extraordinarily simple training. How many times a day, in how many thousands of McDonald's outlets world-wide do you think the phrase "How about French fries?" is asked?

How much money do you think McDonald's makes a day by having each employee say, "How about French fries?" Not very complicated, is it?

**Who's responsible for creating simple "Selling Sentences"
for your most ordinary customer-contact people to say?**

And by the way, it won't hurt to spread a little Recognition, Appreciation and Reward around for your Bs, too. Everybody responds to praise. Just go back to your Psych I Maslow Hierarchy of Human Needs. After Survival and Safety, the third-highest level of human desire is "A Sense of Belonging." Being in some special category. Pull your better workers up and into that category of the "In group"—Belonging, Recognized, Rewarded.

"**Cs**" are to be replaced. Period. Once you hear yourself or your staff arguing whether this person is worth the time you are putting into his training . . . don't waste more training, time, or Empowerment lectures.

This is just plain common sense—and a complete waste of time. Next! Get rid of hopeless "Cs" soon. This week.

FED EX

Federal Express uses a P-S-P philosophy:
People-Service-Profit
People means putting employee concerns first. Involve every employee as an invaluable team member, promote from within, offer outstanding wages, benefits and employee help. Say "thank you" and "well done" often and honestly.

Service means 100% plus. In addition to investing in training, systems and communications, FedEx has created a company culture in which each employee is committed to the 100% standard.

Profit means that every employee must be aware that profit pays for everything and that it all comes from customers. Only profit provides the funds for capital investments, improvements and increased pay.

Produce a short summary of your business mission and develop a way of operating that will guide every employee every day in every customer contact—to act consistently.

WISDOM FROM THE EAST . . .

1. At JCG Finance in Hong Kong, each of the company's 390 employees attends two or three training courses a year. **Forty-two percent** of personnel operating expenses are channeled into skills training.
2. The Oriental Hotel in Bangkok, Thailand is consistently ranked among the top hotels in the world. In an increasingly competitive market, the Oriental is looking to skills of its employees to give it an edge. The hotel holds more than 100 in-house training sessions for its 4,000 employees every year!
3. Development Bank of the Philippines undertook a program of instilling pride and responsibility in its staff through its "shared values" campaign. This involved integrating the metaphor of "the family" into the corporate culture—and encouraging participation and a sense of belonging.

Keeping People and Motivating Them

The Economist (19 March 1994) reports on the positive economic benefits of being nice to workers. Here are some techniques to institutionalize "being nice":

• Properly organized, trained and rewarded teams are generally more productive than individuals working alone. Except for creating art and music, several brains are more likely to solve problems and see the whole picture than one smart head.

- Job security proves to employees that they're valuable and it increases their willingness to take risks. A small equipment distributor taught all his employees how to read his financial statements and discussed the monthly results with them. When business turned down, everyone agreed that instead of firing anyone, all salaries would be cut until business improved—20% for top people, 10% for all others. The company survived. Payroll cuts were restored.

- *The Economist* further reported that companies that are sensitive to their people tie pay to performance and encourage employees to own stock. Employee Stock Ownership Plans are examples. Stock ownership is only one sign of management's trust in and dependence on employees for ideas and customer satisfaction. Studies show companies of all sizes with ESOPs outperform (higher returns on capital and on sales) than comparable non-ESOP firms.

- "Good" companies never stop training. Productivity increases, employees stay where they can grow their skills, value and pay. In-house promotions are a natural consequence of this approach.

- "The Wisdom of Crowds" showed that groups of diverse individuals will almost always make better decisions than single persons—not on technical matters like sugery or engineering—but on sales esimates, options and ideas.

HOWZ BIZNIZ?

Where Have All the Salesmen Gone?

HOW DO THEY STAY IN BUSINESS?

It has long been established that aside from death or a public speech to a thousand people, the most fearful human activity is haggling for the purchase of a new car. That does not apply to Bob Ayrer, an experienced trainer of sales reps. He actually enjoys the buying, negotiating process. Here are two of his true life adventures.

He went out to buy a new company car with a check in his pocket—$18,000—ready to sign over. The first new car dealer he went to was Pete Ellis Dodge.* Bob owed them because they had been sending him business for the glass company where he was Sales VP.

When Bob walked into the showroom at 10:00 AM, he could see the alleged sales people sitting around a desk behind a glass-enclosed office —feet up, drinking coffee, laughing, telling stories.

He walked up to the car in the center of the showroom and began to check it out, opened the doors, got in, popped the trunk, picked up the brochures in the rack next to the car. All of this took about 15 minutes in the middle of their showroom.

When not one of these commission salesmen (?) bothered to come talk to him he left the showroom, drove to Downey Dodge. At Downey he hoped it would be different. The only difference was that there were no sales (?) people in sight—anywhere. Again, after

*Since printing this book, Pete Ellis went bankrupt. But, now he's selling cars via the Internet.

fifteen minutes of self-investigation, poking, looking, examining cars, he left —still with the $18,000, ready-to-spend check snuggled in his pocket. And so went his third stop at a Pontiac dealer. Same total non-interest.

He finally found a Chrysler dealer in another town who would listen to him, hear what he wanted, what price he was ready and able to pay. A check for $18,000 landed right in the dealer's cash register (at that time a top price for that model).

"Here I am, (says Ayrer), a trainer of sales people who emphasizes techniques of Probing and Closing, and these clowns wouldn't take their feet off the desk, put their coffee containers down and *come on out* to talk to a prospect!"

He kept thinking about these incredible experiences and was so bugged he decided to call the Owner or General Manager of the first three dealers he had visited. No one was available. Oh?

Next, he wrote a letter to the head of each of the three dealers he had visited (all had been his customers from the glass company) and never got a single reply or inquiry.

Now we all know other car dealers, especially sales managers, reading this book will shout "Not in my place! My guys are right on the ball every minute!" Okay. We'll see. . . . Although Bob's calls to these dealers failed to raise an Owner or a Manager, he did ask on each call, "How's business?" Every single one said, "Terrible!" No kidding. Too bad. Can't imagine why . . .

WE WORK FOR NOTHING

Office Machine Repair Service in New York—Delson Business Systems. A small Sharp copier needed service. Man called Delson to schedule a service call in his apartment home/office, but emphasized: not to send anyone unless they call first. (His wife receives patients in her clinical psychology practice at this apartment.)

The repairman showed up without a prior call (swell) but, fortunately, no patient was there. However, his wife had to leave in a short while, leaving the so-called serviceman there alone. The serviceman was rude, spent time using the phone, did not explain the reason for the repair, and left both the machine and the lights on in the apartment when he left.

Man called to complain about service. When the invoice came the owner sent it back unpaid with a note that it would remain unpaid until someone called to respond to his complaint about the service. Between the first invoice and a second request for payment, the company sent a questionnaire on "Quality of Service"—which was sent back with a repeated description of the complaint. No one called. A third request for payment arrived. Man sent the same note—"No money until someone calls." Three months have passed. No money has been sent. No calls have been received.

Wonder who their accountants are?

OPEN-DOOR SALES POLICY?

Thanks to the great California Northridge Earthquake, homeowners in this area had to become experts in constructing and contracting. After meeting with five different general contractors, all of whom either didn't have time, or wanted him to mortgage his family for the next three generations, Jeff Newby bit the bullet and decided to be his own general contractor.

His favorite story involves the patio doors: Like most 1960s houses, his had aluminum sliding doors. His wife, Trish, has forever wanted wooden French doors. And she had exact specifications— one was to be a six-foot sliding French door and the other to be two French doors, opening out, with sidelights (small opening windows with screens) which opened in.

Jeff decided that satisfying his wife with her unusual doors was much easier and less painful than the alternatives—a disastrous marriage, divorce, or a lifetime of scorn. After visiting a few high-priced distributors, he now had all the information he needed to visit the local building supply warehouse. "I wouldn't want to name that store," he said, "but I always thought that depots were where trains stopped."

The first time he shopped there for doors he dealt with a seasoned salesman who wore a carpenter's belt loaded with tools. (Badges of professionalism? Or stage dressing?) Jeff told him what he wanted, to which the salesman replied:

"This is what I've got."

"Well," Jeff replied, "that's not what I asked for."

"I don't have what you asked for," was the response.

"Okay, how long would it take to order what I want?"

"Eight to ten weeks."

"Well, I really need them sooner than that," visualizing the open walls in the middle of the construction project. "When will you have more regular stock in?"

"Eight to ten weeks," he said again.

"But don't you re-stock more often than that?" Jeff asked incredulously.

The so-called salesman then answered with a non sequitur. "We're very busy." And added his own personal customer service compliment: "Why don't you get a contractor who knows what he's doing?"

Defeated, Jeff departed.

PLAY IT AGAIN, SAM

A couple of days later Jeff returned and made a point to find a different salesman. This man was very helpful, not insulting, and went out of his way to try and satisfy Jeff. However, the supplier was the salesman's undoing. While he was right in front of Jeff and the rep from the door factory was on the phone, this was the conversation:

"Making doors that open out is a special order."

"Can you make sidelights that open in combined with a door that can open *out?*"

"No, it's impossible to make doors that open out and sidelights that open in."

Jeff asked a simple question through the helpful salesman: "Why?"

"Because that's the way it's done."

"Can't they make a special order for me that works the way I want?"

"No!"

Suddenly the factory's salesman did have some good news. "Tell your customer," he relayed through the now exasperated salesman, "that we can deliver regular stock in only four weeks."

In other words, I would get the order *I didn't want* in less time than the order I did want.

QUESTION: How is your Custom Service?
How do your people handle requests out of the ordinary?

FAKED OUT

The Barnes & Noble mail order catalogue described a "fake book"—shorthand musical clues for playing piano lyrics, abbreviated melody and chords. Man stopped at three B&N stores in Manhattan. None had the book. *No one offered to take his name, order, and mail the book.*

Man then called the Barnes & Noble main office number, asked for the fake book, was kept on hold for four minutes, hung up, called again. The same clerk asked where he'd gone. (Interesting reaction or clever sales technique.)

They had no system to determine what was in inventory so she had checked the shelves, but didn't tell the customer where she was going or what she was doing. **Always tell the Customer what you're doing. Does wonders to cut down customer frustration!** No fake book—the reason was that it was available only through mail order. OK—would she take his name, address, and credit card and send it? No, she couldn't do that, but she would give him the mail order 800 number.

He told her he didn't *want* to make any more calls. He *wanted* to give B & N his money NOW. Why was she making that so hard to do? She said, "You sound upset . . . " He agreed that he was too upset to make still another phone call and we could forget all about his giving B & N the business.

SAME COMPANY—DIFFERENT STORY

And yet . . . in Pasadena, California the Barnes & Noble people couldn't be more accommodating. Yes, they can locate the book you're looking for here in the store. Yes, they can special order. And Yes! They will match any discount price competitors offer.

Plus . . . they have a Starbucks Coffee shop inside the B&N store where you can sit, sip and scan books you might be interested in buying. And no scolding about spilling coffee on an unbought book!

Is this difference in attitude because Pasadena is a new Barnes & Noble? Does management send their best people to open a new store? (We doubt it.) Is New York just jaded?

Or is it a systems failure?

LUCK OF THE DRAW

Does brand-store-product loyalty depend on "who you get" to serve you?

How often have we all experienced this kind of argument?

I say, "American is the greatest."

You say, "I wouldn't fly American if they gave me the seat next to the pilot!"

Reason? I had terrific experiences with American. The flight attendant upgraded me. My Walkman headset broke and the flight engineer found one for me on board. My passport was stolen in London and one of the American executives led me right through the customs routine and got me back to the States. I love American! On the other hand, you had a lousy experience with American—for whatever reasons, hate it, wouldn't fly it for free.

QUESTION: Should Customer Service—and Customer Retention depend so much on the "luck of the draw?" Should my loyalty be due to the one person I happen to get as my service person?

**Attitude and enthusiasm should be universal
in your company. Training and constant
surveillance for lurking
WAYMISHes are a must.**

Measuring, Monitoring and Short Term Goals—

The answers to providing *consistent* service:

<hr>

Suggestions from "Productivity Views" on improving customer satisfaction:

1. Forty percent of service costs come from *redoing* work, so doing it right in the first place saves money. Perform detailed systems analyses, test systems, constantly improve your systems.
2. Tie your business goal to daily quantity, quality and customer satisfaction measures. Self-reporting lets each person know the results of the work immediately. Basic rule for process, service and profit improvement: (1) Get people to agree on what is acceptable, exceptional performance. (2) Let them know how they're doing. (3) Get out of their way and let them make any corrections.
3. Get everyone involved in the improvement process. Supervisors probably know 10 to 20 small ways to cut costs for every large cost-cutting measure top management initiates. And small improvements are faster, easier, safer, more acceptable than the big ones. The Japanese call this concept KAIZEN.

<hr>

Ask for the Order (AFTO)

If your company performs a service, or sells a product (is there a company that doesn't?) train your employees—consistently, throughout the organization—in the AFTO mentality. So many companies miss opportunities to use Selling Sentences to make a sale.

A motorist stops at a gas station just asking for directions. Train the attendants to say . . . "How about some gas and a clean windshield while you're here. Just take a minute . . . " Customers love suggestions.

A pedestrian strolls into a bookshop. "Feel free to browse, madam, and we have coffee and cakes over here if you'd like." Fact: The longer we keep the customer here, the better the chance she will buy.

RETAIL STORE: Shopper hesitates near a clothing display. "Try on anything you like. There's no charge for that"—and with a smile indicate your special sale prices for this week. People love to brag about "the bargain I got today."

RESTAURANT: We made a personal bet with a friend-owner that if every server used this sentence: "You really ought to try our creme brulee dessert today (tonight), it's terrific"—dessert business would double. (It tripled.)

Think about McDonald's remarkably simple, automatic add-on phrase: "How about French fries?" Those four words sell millions of extra French fries every day.

National Sanitary (janitorial) Supply's phone room order-takers ask, "How are you fixed for tissue, towels, and hand soap?" Ordinarily, these three items are give-away, loss-leaders to get in the door. With those ten words National adds another $10,000 a week in sales—and books the orders at retail prices!

Ask for the order! Add Selling Sentences! Train your people WHAT TO SAY.

Here's What to Say

AUTO REPAIR SHOP: "You know, Mr. Cohn, if you'd let me rotate those tires on a regular schedule you could probably get a heck of a lot more wear out of them and save some money . . . " And what will be Mr. Cohn's first choice when the time comes to buy his *new* tires?

JEWELRY STORE: "If you have any anniversaries or birthdays coming up, you can pick out some jewelry now and use our lay-away plan. That way you only pay a little at a time over a couple of months . . . " It's the Plan-Ahead sale.

HOTEL: "We have a new separate concierge floor. You get this special elevator key, free cocktails in the evening in our concierge lounge, continental breakfast . . . and this entire upgrade only costs ten dollars more—which you will save in food and drinks alone."

We said YES (and added that piece of Marriott's training to our Selling Sentences category.)

We're sure you get the idea: Find the easiest "add-on" sentence you can create, teach it to everybody. Ask For The Order—constantly.

Change the add-on sentence occasionally so it's not boring. Count the extra profits as they roll in.

AFTO—creatively used—can work in any business!
Special offer: Send us a challenge. We'll help you create some
AFTO phrases for your business.

Incidentally, "Mr. Retail" is Stanley Marcus, the patriarch Chairman of Neiman-Marcus, an inveterate shopper and a super sales-minded merchant. For one year he kept score of the merchandise he was interested in buying from stores other than his own. What he didn't buy (but would have) amounted to $46,734 dollars. All because no sales person **asked for the order.**

NO ROOM AT THE INN

On a slightly arrogant presumption, a salesman went to busy Santa Barbara on a major holiday weekend without a reservation, feeling that with his super persuasive talents he could always talk his way into a room. He'd done it many times before.

But—the entire resort town was booked solid. After a round of 5 or 6 major hotels, the now deflated salesman entered Fess Parker's gigantic Red Lion Inn (now owned by Double Tree), looking crestfallen, reduced to begging for space. A tall grey-haired man in chino pants and saddle shoes standing in the lobby scanning and surveying the milling holiday arrivals, correctly interpreted the frustrated look of the salesman. Extending his hand, the man said, "You look like you've got a serious problem. Let's see if we can help." [How's *that* for a sales opening sentence?]

Turned out this was the Manager of the hotel, Jim Buckley, retired from Marriott, re-drafted for the Red Lion. Jim tried in vain to carve out one more room here in his hotel. Nothing, the staff assured him. Honest, Mr. Buckley, absolutely no space, not even in the broom closet.

Shaking his head, Jim called two of his staff and instructed them: "Call everywhere in town and please—get a room for this man." (Wow!

How often would this happen?)

Twenty-one calls later the energetic staff reported the only space available was at the Ojai Inn, 38 miles back toward Los Angeles. The salesman, also a writer, was grateful, went to his car, returned with a copy of his book, *The Great Brain Robbery*, and offered it autographed to Manager Jim as a Thank You for this extraordinary courtesy.

Lesson in response and selling: One week later, the salesman got a handwritten card from the Red Lion saying, "I read your book. Enjoyed it. Next time—remember—always book in advance and *stay with us!*" Included were his business card, and an added handwritten personal phone extension.

Former employer Arthur R. Greene used to say as he scanned your business correspondence: *"Good, but where's the sell?"*

Jim Buckley knows about selling and AFTO = Ask For The Order. Every time.

How to tell how you're doing

SUGGESTION: Develop standards that are measurable—and reported daily.

—percent of orders filled
—percent of orders shipped
—transactions entered into the computer the same day
—how you are handling customer complaints
—daily use of a Nurturing technique to keep the customers you have

EXAMPLE:

A photo album manufacturer based its business on fast and complete order deliveries to K-Mart, WalMart, and down to the local photo stores.

Every morning, workers looked at a large chart as they came through the door. There was yesterday's performance compared to the standard, the prior day's and the month-to-date.

At the first coffee break, an extra five minutes was spent on analyzing the variances and deciding how to get back to 100%.

P.S. Bonuses are company-wide and based on achieving production and quality goals.

Everybody knows. Everybody works. Everybody wins.

CUSTOMERS FOR LIFE

THE ODDS ARE UNBELIEVABLE

THE LEGENDARY Connecticut grocery firm Stew Leonard's has the highest sales per square foot in the United States. The stores (there are three,) each serve 100,000 customers a week! Their fabulous customer service has made the pages of newspapers and magazines across the country, won service awards and been touted on video tapes. Their reputation has drawn most major companies in the country to come look at **How They Do It**. You would think the owners would be fat, happy and satisfied. Not so!

In one of their weekly newsletters, there was a most fascinating statistic saying . . . "If we lose only **1/100th of 1 percent** of our 100,000 customers a week"—(hardly worth mentioning you would think) . . . "and the average shopping bill of each of our 100,000 customers is $100 a week . . . our stores would lose $2,500,000 a year!"

Extending those numbers out over a ten year period, the stores would suffer a **$25 MILLION DOLLAR** loss in future business from the customers lost in that first year!

Here is the frightening math: Lose just 10 customers a week = 500 lost customers a year. That 500 x $5,000 (50 weeks x $100) = $2,500,000 a year!!!

THE LESSON:

Their unbelievably focused Customer Attention record is light years ahead of most American businesses in dramatic customer-focused service. Yet this store drums into its employees—and management—how that infinitesimal 1/100th of 1 percent (less than two customers a day), can make a multi-million dollar difference over time!

And the loss can be as inconsequential as one moment's rudeness by one unthinking employee.

To Consider

How can your business set up WAYMISH screens—warning signals—so employees are trained to immediately detect the slightest CUSTOMER DISSATISFACTION?

Can you empower them to Do Whatever They Have To Do . . . to make it right for that disappointed customer . . . and KEEP THE CUSTOMER?

TO FURTHER CONSIDER . . .

• Have you calculated the Lifetime Value of your customer?
• How can you impress all your employees with what one lost customer can mean to your future sales?
• Please . . . do your "multiplication": the money you lose long term from a short term mistake can be frightening.

OUR PROMISE TO YOU:

It will absolutely positively pay to get a handle on the Lifetime Value of your customer. Calculators are cheap. Lost customers are not.

SUGGESTION:
Create a New Executive Title — Immediately

There should be a new position created in every sales-driven company; a Manager in Charge of **Keeping** Customers!

Appoint one person in your company who is constantly checking, asking and uncovering WAYMISH problems that have happened . . . and those about to happen . . . to teach your people what they could have done, or what to say or do . . . next time.

POINT:

Keeping and recapturing existing customers is THE cheapest way to increase business and profits.

[Betcha a Manager in Charge of Keeping Customers would pay for him/herself in six months.]

Kindly Quiz for the Marketing Folk:

Is it not true . . . as a business, you have extensive customer records? (Yes.) You know who's buying? (Yes.) What about assigning some bright soul to the case of those NOT buying? (Please.) Where are our Missing Customers? Why aren't they buying from us?

ONE WAY TO DO IT

Dodsworth's restaurant on a Saturday night. Customer suddenly remembers seeing a Diners Club booklet listing four local restaurants, including this one, offering a 20% discount for using the special Le Card from Diners.

Customer introduces self to owner. He is not a friend or even close acquaintance, but his cheery greeting and welcoming handshake show he understands Sales and Customer Service.

"Say," customer begins, "I'm sure (emphasis on sure), just today I saw . . . " and describes the offer. Owner smiles broadly: "Ha! I haven't even talked to Diners for over a year but if you say it's in the book I believe you and I'll see you get the discount. What amount did they say?"

Twenty percent. "Fine!" he says. He claps customer on the back and turns away as he says, "Thanks for coming in!"

At the end of the meal the customer tells the waiter the deal, tips on the gross (only fair) and leaves.

Later he discovers by reading the fine print in Le Card's promotion, the 20% is deducted by Diners Club at invoicing time. Oops. But you know the customer will favor this place and not just once. The owner knows how to operate, how to make it pleasant, and practices making it EASY for people to give him their money.

Go With the Numbers

- It's five times more expensive to get a new customer than to keep the one you have.
- 55-77% of customers will do business with you again—if you handle their complaints, inquiries and requests *promptly*.
- 95% of customers will do business with you again if you handle their complaints and requests for information IMMEDIATELY.

(From John Goodman's TARP study)

Please read these figures again and think hard about how FAST your company responds to requests for information . . . inquiries . . . and handling complaints.

$90,000 HERE—$90,000 THERE . . .

Louise Borchert handled payroll at Lochridge & Company, a Boston-based consulting company. After many years of using a local CPA firm to do the payroll, Louise switched to ADP. Good reputation. Major company. Figured there would be no problem. Lochridge had approximately 25 employees. How difficult could it be?

In eight months (that's eight straight attempts) ADP got the payroll correct once. One out of eight times. Good odds? That would be .125, a marginal batting average even in the minor leagues.

But the most incredible news follows.

Lochridge hired a new employee mid-month. His paycheck for the partial month should have been $900. (That's nine *hundred*.) ADP sent the new employee eleven paychecks for $90,000 (ninety *thousand*) **each.** Eleven checks, each made out for $90,000 for the same employee! Is that generous—or what? A $989,100 gigantic goof.

Fortunately, Louise caught the mistake. "Not only did ADP have no Quality Control" Louise reports, "they wouldn't even admit they had made a mistake." Nor did they ever acknowledge her calls or letter. ADP didn't even acknowledge Louise when she canceled the contract.

Another good company with an incredibly costly WAYMISH loses a perfectly good customer because of a hidden mistake—a goof some employee has never admitted. (ADP management is probably discovering this horror for the first time as they read this.)

(Repeat thought, but so important): How much better to have an "It's OK to make a mistake" atmosphere in a company—apologize to the customer from and to the right level—and KEEP THE CUSTOMER.

This Could Help You

Here are seven steps that will reduce your costs handling customer service problems:

1. Fix problems *on the spot*
   (Permit *empowerment* and use Nike's advice: Just Do It!)
2. *Don't* start writing form letters about "Call our office . . ."
   (That's an excuse for not solving the problem.)
3. *Stop* the paper trail before it starts.
   (Why keep staff busy with a non-profit Paper Chase?)
4. Solve it now.
   (Lose a little profit; keep the customer; move on!)
5. Teach employees the C.A.L.M. technique.
   Stay **C**ool. **A**pologize. **L**isten. **M**ake it Right.
      (Credit: Carol Christison, International Deli Dairy Association)
6. Ask the customer what you can do to improve service.
   (And reduce the chance of this problem happening again.)
7. Take the long view. Keep the customer and future profits.

(This doesn't mean giving in to every customer's wish. Ted's philosopher father-in-law used to say, "Count to 10 before saying NO—unless life or limb is involved.") Only the rare off-the-wall customer request should be denied.

Reward: For Return of Lost Customers!

How often have you been called or contacted by any company after you stopped doing business with them?

Has the manager, owner or executive of a store, catalog, medical office, health club, restaurant or any business called and said, "Where are you? What happened? We want you back!"

Wouldn't you as an ex-customer be eager to tell your WAYMISH story, wait for a reasonable response and if satisfied, return to the fold?

The Professors Speak: The Value of Keeping Customers

(*Harvard Business Review*, Sept.-Oct. 1990—and still good advice)

After investing in the costs of acquiring a customer, a firm expects to make a profit on the base volume. Continued customer loyalty increases this base profit from higher purchases and, in the case of credit, higher balances and added income from the interest charges.

At the next level, continued customer relationships reduce operating costs—sales and customer service people become more efficient in handling the customer, partnership deals are developed: customers and the firm benefit from frequent-buying programs or annual-purchase contracts and shared savings.

Long-term customers are, by definition, happy and a rich source of referrals. They're also more aware of the superior service they're getting and are receptive to higher prices for the perceived value.

Academic language and good advice to say—

KEEP THE CUSTOMER—IT PAYS ALL WAYS!

BUT . . . EVEN THE BIG GUYS MISS

One Corporate Commitment That Didn't Work

"Ask me why I gave up my American Express card . . . " was the first message we received after we requested our friends to send in WAYMISH stories. This was a customer with a high-end platinum American Express card.

Around year's end, he called American Express and asked, "Hello!? Where's my new card, please?"

"Being sent in the mail," they said.

He waits. Something he is not good at.

A week goes by. He calls. Their reply (a little testy), "It was sent." Ten days more. No card.

It's now three weeks into January, he calls for the third time, "Where is my platinum card, **Please**?"

Customer Service woman snaps, "We've sent you three already! You must have them!"

Our platinum card customer is a direct-mail executive and computer literate. "Do me a favor," he says, "pull up my screen and tell me how much my record shows I've charged on your card in the last weeks of December and January . . . "

Answer: "Well . . . just a moment . . . Nothing . . . No charges . . . B-b-b-but we sent THREE cards!"

"I haven't gotten any. Not one," says Platinum Man.

"Well," scolds the so-called Customer Service Rep, "that's not our fault! We couldn't have missed mailing them."

The Customer smiled, "You know what? For the last three weeks I haven't missed you either." And hangs up.

What kind of loss, you might ask, will this WAYMISH cost American Express?

Well, last year this high-placed, client-entertaining executive racked up $40,000 on his credit cards. Couldn't the Customer Rep see this from the records?

QUESTION: Is it better for an employee to have the satisfaction of "putting a customer in his place" or . . . can we get our people to focus on this customer problem and realize they should do *whatever they have to do* to save the account?

At 40 grand a pop, what's the question???

Just Suppose . . .

. . . You were the AmEx customer service manager, and you had a Reward System that motivated your reps to report any high volume "Important Lost Account" . . . with absolutely no recrimination or penalty to the rep.

TEST: Think right now—As an AmEx executive, what would you do to get this Platinum cardholder back? Easy answer, huh?

Anyone reading this book would know to pick up the phone, identify yourself and your title and "make a deal" to make it right.

QUESTION: Then how come companies don't do that? Is it because the top level doesn't know what the bottom level is doing?

Or does the bottom level dare not tell the top level about mistakes for fear of losing their job?

Ah, well. Big company. Small loss. One customer.

HAVE YOUR PEOPLE CALL MY PEOPLE

An instructor of a direct-mail class, intrigued with the unusual catalogs from the J. Peterman Co., decided to call Peterman and get samples to demonstrate a top-class catalog to his students.

The J. Peterman Co. was known for fine customer service. The instructor knew this first-hand from a personal experience with Peterman when they made a generous merchandise exchange for him.

Instructor called the Kentucky number listed in the catalog. The Peterman people who answered the phone didn't have the foggiest idea as to whether they could send catalogs. (Then what are catalogs for?) But they suggested the instructor call back.

So he hesitated and said, "You want me to make a second long-distance call when I am trying to help your company? This is to your benefit."

"They" couldn't handle that. Or wouldn't take the responsibility to make a decision to handle or pass along a simple customer request. Or promise to have someone from Peterman call back. What would it cost to call back? Fifty cents? A dollar? A WATS line charge?

Here is another situation where our favored phrase could quickly solve the problem:

SURE . . . I CAN HANDLE THAT FOR YOU.

Isn't it interesting that no matter how skilled a company is generally (and corporately) at delivering top-notch excellence in Customer Service (which J. Peterman was), some person down the line either (a) didn't get the Customer Service message, (b) decided to make the decision of "what I think is right" (but not necessarily for the Company), or (c) hasn't been adequately trained in the Company's real mission—to Get and Keep Customers.

Right People in the Right Places

SERVICE QUESTION: Can any company afford to stop training/selling all of their people on the one precious concept that the Customer is "right" and that the Customer is the Number One reason they are in business?

No. Not ever. Not for one day, one week or in answering one phone call.

Maybe there are people on your phones who don't like customers but are quite capable in other parts of their job.

Innovative Idea: The President of one Southern California company dictated this rule:

If you don't *like* to talk on the phone, you are no longer permitted to *answer* the phone!

DO I SHARE A ROOM
OR NOT?

A man had confirmed a late arrival reservation the night before a convention speech at the Atlanta Hyatt. Arrived at 10 PM. The reservation clerk said there was no room—but he'd arrange a room in a nearby hotel.

Why was there no room for a confirmed reservation? Their explanation: A guest who was supposed to leave had changed her mind and legally the hotel couldn't force her to leave.

The next morning the angry, displaced guest called Hilton, Marriott, Sheraton and the office of the Georgia Attorney General to see what the law was. In each case he asked: "If I had a reservation for *Tuesday* night only and decided I wanted to stay through Wednesday night, and another guest had a confirmed reservation for Wednesday night, who, legally, had the right to the room?" In ALL cases, the answer was the person with the *Wednesday* night reservation. Our frustrated friend then went to the Hyatt manager.

Faced with this information—with the guest knowing that he'd been lied to—the Hyatt manager apologized and offered a pair of Hyatt cuff links to make up for the mistake.

The cuff links would constantly remind the frustrated guest of this debacle. The offer was refused. (What should the Hyatt manager have offered instead?) A letter to Hyatt's head office brought no response.

The Hyatt manager could have appeased the guest with a free meal, or free limo ride to the airport, or even a free night at any Hyatt. The manager had lied; he needed to do something substantive to restore Hyatt's reputation.

DILEMMA: Does the hotel throw out the over-staying guest and lose *her* as a customer? Or refuse the confirmed reservation and lose *him* as a customer? Does each scenario need to breed a well-poisoner for that hotel or the chain?

Anybody out there got the answer?

ARE YOU PLAYING THE PERCENTAGES?

(Sports and Business combined)

The difference between companies is getting smaller. The competition is obviously tougher. In the language of sports stats:

The gap between a .265 batter in baseball and one with a .315 average is only **5%, or one more hit in twenty times at bat**.

The difference between professional tour golfers and scratch handicap golfers who never make the grade is *one stroke for each 18 hole round*.

The top 25 tennis players hit the ball about *one inch sooner* than the rest of their competitors—hardly measurable but very significant in timing, power, accuracy and tournaments won.

And . . . in business or sports, the closer you get to the top, the more difficult it is to keep improving. (The law of diminishing returns.)

Maybe checking these 4 points will help.

1. Analysis of what is needed and wanted,
2. Statistical controls of how you're doing,
3. Participation from everyone, and
4. Using "just plain common sense."

"Yes, yes," you say. "We do that."

Good! Combine these points with true customer focus and you're rare—now you've definitely increased your odds and your competitive advantage!

LET'S HAVE A TREASURE HUNT

Customer orders shoes at J.C. Penney, is told they are not in stock, come back in four days. Customer does.

CLERK: What did you order?

CUS: Casual Shoe, size 10 beige.

CLERK: Who did you talk to?

CUS: I dunno . . .

CLERK: Well then how can I help if you don't know?

CUS: Did you get a shipment of shoes?

CLERK: Yeah—they're back in the closet.

CUS: Could you get mine?

CLERK: What do they look like?

CUS: They're a size 10, beige walking shoe . . .

CLERK: Well—best I can do is show you where they are . . .

She proceeds to take customer to stock room where there are piles of boxes.

CLERK: These are from a pretty recent shipment, I think. Why don't you go through those boxes and see if you can find yours?

This must be a new twist in Self Service: "Go into the closet and help yourself . . . "

J. C. Penney, the wonderful Old Man who started all these good stores, was a Customer Service fanatic. His fervor for near perfection had him ask his salesmen: "Are you sure you've polished the back of your shoes?"

Sloppy, thoughtless service coming out of the closet like this must have poor old James Cash Penney revolving rapidly in his grave.

POINT: Are you inviting your customers to report lousy service?

If not, and you were the manager of this store, how would you know who's killing your future sales? WAYMISHes are alive and squirming—out on the sales floor and in the closet.

AN ACE UP THE SLEEVE

Man and his wife were shopping in the Costa Mesa, California Nordstrom store. It was Christmas Season and the store was VERY busy, as Nordstrom stores usually are.

They had already made a few purchases and were pawing over shirts. She wondered out loud, "What sleeve length are Steve's arms?"—their 6'6" son-in-law.

"Use the phone over here!" came the crisp, brisk, polite offer from a stylish young lady just behind them. "It's a San Francisco call," the man warned her. (A 350-mile long-distance call.)

"Do you know the number?" she asked coolly, as she headed behind the counter.

"Uh huh," the man said, bedazzled by this instant open invitation. He checked his pocket address book. "Dial 9 first!" she tossed over her shoulder as she handed him the phone and went on speaking to her staff.

He called, got the neck and sleeve size, ordered the shirt and laughed. His wife looked puzzled and asked, "What's funny?"

"For a 75-cent phone call they wrap up a $50 order, the shirt and me! I can't imagine trying to make a long-distance call from any other store."

Another Nordstrom "just do it" legend.

THE FINE ART OF KNOWING

Jack Abelson was a manufacturer of fine jewelry. Hardly a Harvard MBA, he'd had two years of formal schooling and was out on the streets of New York at the age of eight. He sold on long-term credit but not on consignment. And he had that rare gift: an intuitive sense of customer relationships.

Jack had a little ritual. After a long day of buying, selling, negotiating, he would sit back and have one drink of Scotch—often sharing the time with a friend who dropped by. One night after business hours, the phone rang and his visitor heard this: "Not a problem, not at all. I understand. Just send it back."

The fact was the customer on the phone had bought some merchandise three years ago for about $5000 and now wanted to return it as "unsaleable." Jack accepted the goods, issued a credit (after three years) and told the customer he was happy to be of service.

Lesson: Jack *knew* that the customer *knew* the goods were perfectly saleable. But Jack knew the customer needed the money or further credit. Did Jack make a mistake? Not at all. He knew and the customer knew exactly what was going on. Jack let his customer save face. And now this customer was tied to Jack by one of those wonderful unspoken, unsigned pacts that help hold on to customers for life.

**Intuitively or not, it makes no sense to lose
a customer over an argument or claim . . . does it?**

GOOD STUFF

WAY TO GO! A PRO!

AT THE Miami Beach Saks Fifth Avenue store, a shopper was looking for some travel-friendly shirts—spun nylon that looked good after washing and without ironing. The mature attentive sales lady could not find any on the display tables, but thought there might be some in the storeroom. The inventory boy was out for lunch, could the customer wait until she checked? "Why not shop around the store and come back in ten minutes," she suggested.

Agreed. Ten minutes later, flustered, hair unkempt, but with a triumphant look, the accommodating clerk showed him spun nylon shirts in blue, yellow, white, and pink. He bought two blues, a white, and a yellow and, as he tells it: "When I was leaving I remembered a book which suggested saying an honest 'Thank You' to someone every day.

"I decided to do that. So I walked back to her and said 'You're a real pro—a first-rate sales person. I appreciate your extra effort.' She blushed, smiled, obviously pleased with my compliment but the surprising thing was . . . I felt better!"

Who does not respond to compliments . . . when deserved?

RECOMMENDED: Try this One-a-day *Thank You* plan.

If you are observant, at least one of the people you work with, are in contact with, buy from, sell to, deal with, deserves a "tip of the hat" for going the extra mile in Attitude.

Tell them you noticed!

There are a lot of ways to do this:

One short compliment in person . . . a 12-second phone message . . . a scrawled 10 to 12 word Thank You or "attaboy" on small note paper . . . Be specific: Not "Thanks for the good job" but "Thanks for being patient (imaginative, thoughtful) with that customer."

There was a wonderful story about a man named Gilbert who was President of a company in St. Louis. He used to write dozens of tiny notes every day—"Good job!" "Appreciate your concern for our customers." "We're certainly glad you're here!"—and then at the end of the afternoon he would personally deliver them to the mail room.

One of his staff snickered, "He delivers the notes himself because he's ashamed of writing so many." "No, no, no," reported Mr. Gilbert's long-time secretary, "he goes to the mail room so he can see, say Hello to, and tell the mail room what an important job they're doing for the company." (Did some one mention Motivation?)

A champion of this small-note technique was George Zahka at the old Dickie-Raymond agency in Boston. When you were there six months, a note would arrive on that date with a handwritten "Glad you're with us. Keep up the good work," on one of those 4 x 5-inch office pads. At the one-year mark, another, differently worded note. On your birthday, same size paper, same familiar neat handwriting. Truth: you never got tired of George's "little notes." Over the years, they forged a strong personal link between an excellent manager and a good friend.

HOW DO THOSE GUYS DO THAT?

The paragon of retailers, Nordstrom, opened a new anchor store in a well-to-do mall. They offered valet parking at the front door. Valet parking at a department store? Uh huh. Just like John Wanamaker's original 1800s store in Philadelphia when Mr. Wanamaker had a frocked and tasseled livery man to park the carriages . . . for the carriage trade, of course.

The original Nordic emigrant Nordstroms were shoe people and, as such, were very close to the customer. (How much closer can you get than kneeling down in front of a lady and slipping various shoe styles and sizes upon her feet?) So both the attitude and the attention of Nordstrom sales people remain as the family Nordstrom began— genteel, polite, with a nothing-is-too-much-trouble attitude.

Nordstrom is a total service (super service) department store. Even buying shoes there is an experience. You see handsome, bright, young, well-dressed sales associates hustling quickly to and from the stock rooms, their chins balancing a stack of boxes cradled in their arms as they pivot nimbly through the crowded aisles. And the key word is Hustling. You can sense the energy in Nordstrom.

Says salesman Sean with enthusiasm, "Do we have this in stock? Yes!" (And they do know their stock.) "I also have that shoe in turquoise, and while I get it, why don't I bring the low heel in both the blue and the navy?" (Up-selling.) And he is off swiftly to the doorway of the stock room. Meantime in the background, a tuxedo-clad pianist is playing lyrical chords of "The Phantom of the Opera" theme as some shoppers tarry to watch and listen. Class act, Nordstrom.

Salesman Sean returns. Talks. Describes. Encourages. Suggests. "I know I can get both of these styles from our other stores in a day or two—and even if I'm not here, I'll have one of my colleagues call you when they arrive." (Won't be here? Where is Sean going?) To be with his wife when she has their first baby expected two days from now, he announces beaming with pride.

One pair of shoes was bought and carried away that day. Word that the other pair was ready to be picked up came via a handwritten note from Sean dated on the day he was with wife, miles away at the hospital!

A few, very few people know how to Do It Right. Sean is one. Nordstrom has a host of them. And you might ask, like the

Sundance Kid asked, "How do those guys do that?" Translation: Where do they find these people? They look for *Attitude*. Nordstrom takes the time to hire the right people— which proves, there *are* these rare bright, alert sales people *with the right attitude out there*. And they will work for you—if you choose well, pay well, don't smother them with infantile fraidy-cat rules, but treat them like mature adults who know how to deal with grown people.

THE RETURN OF SEAN

Four months go by . . . December, January, February, March 18. A Saturday shopping tour once more to Nordstrom (same store in Arcadia, California).

Remembering the positive impression of four months ago, the husband of the lady shoe shopper is curious. He asks if Sean was still in the department. "I'm Sean," says the smiling young Nordstromite.

"How's the baby?" says the husband recovering.

"Wonderful!" he beams, "and your wife is with you?"

"Right there," says the man pointing.

Man is hailed by a male friend shopping. Shakes hands. They talk. The ladies shop.

Seeing a different shoe salesman than Sean writing up the new shoe order, the man asks, "Why not give the sale to your friend Sean?"

Wife answers: "Oh, he doesn't sell any more. He's the supervisor of the whole shoe section now."

"Did you talk to him?"

"Yes, he came over and asked me how I liked the emerald and navy 10B's with the nail-head design I bought in November."

NOVEMBER! EGAD! How's that for memory? Attention to customers? Focus?

It's all part of the Nordstrom secret: TCOB—Taking Care of Business . . . and the customer.

THE PALATCHINKENS

After a movie, four couples stopped for a bite at the Claremont Diner, a suburban New Jersey restaurant, and ordered eight palatchinkens (large pancake-like crepes) for which the Diner was famous. A waitress brought out only seven plates. She apologized to the eighth person. Mr. Bauman, one of the owners of the restaurant, she explained, had checked the eight palatchinkens and didn't like the way one looked. A new one would be ready in a few minutes—at NO CHARGE. Each of the eight people in the group was suitably impressed and has re-told the story of the eighth palatchinken to countless people.

Business or Ballyhoo?

Was "number 8" really a bad palatchinken or was it the mark of a shrewd marketer?

Regardless . . . Our repeated advice to anyone dedicated to Pleasing and Keeping Customers: your product is often *the* cheapest thing you can give away. You **know** exactly what it costs.

Think about "giving it away" occasionally. It might be the very best way to create a mini-legend for your customers to pass on to friends, Romans and countrymen.

HOOKED ON CELLULAR

Cellular phones are a necessity in the freeway madness of Los Angeles, where every hour is Rush Hour traffic. And to operate sensibly and continuously, you do need two batteries for your mobile phone. One charging while the other's in use. I had only one battery and my phone went dead.

AirTouch Cellular has a magnificent Customer Service/Sales team between Lane Moore, super salesman with a voice that should be heard on national TV and Terri Radek, an "anything-you-want" service lady.

When my phone went out, I called Lane who said with that smile in his voice, "Put it in the mail, Ray, and by FedEx tomorrow, we'll have you a loaner." Next morning—bingo! New phone and batteries (plural) while my "down" phone was still en route to Lane and Terri.

Ah—but when the units arrived, there was what super clothier Max Grassfield calls "the finishing touch." Small Post-Its were stuck on each unit, handwritten. "Ray—this needs to be charged when new for 12 hours the first time, then eight hours is fine to recharge. T." (Terri Radek). Isn't that a neat idea? Who reads all that micro-sized fine print in those eye-straining instruction booklets? Here, Terri tells you the whole deal in one handwritten sentence. Nice touch.

That got my attention and then I saw one more Post-It (different color): "Yell if you need help. LM."

**Take heed, shippers of product, on the How To's
of building Customers for Life.**

GRACIOUS MONEY

For whose benefit are store-open hours set? Gracious Home, a Manhattan retailer offering just about everything you need in your home, opens at 9 AM. A customer about to leave his apartment for a month realized he hadn't bought camphor anti-moth protecting material. He called Gracious Home at 7:45 AM and luckily reached the manager, who, hearing the story, said, "Come right over!"

The anti-moth camphor was ready and waiting. The manager gave the customer his personal number and told him to use it anytime he needed help. Where does the customer go for everything he needs in his home without thinking about shopping for price?

People rarely buy for price alone. They also buy satisfaction. Personal association. Assurance. Comfort. And sometimes, from a sense of appreciation of past service.

Power of the Pen

In this day of computerized everything, there is no way to tell where or how the personalized note or letter you got was generated. Very tricky, these computers.

But there is a way to be different: The handwritten note.

A great selling tool, especially for the superior sales person, regardless of what product or service is being offered.

Harvey Mackay, the Swim with the Sharks author, beats the drum steadily for quick hand-jotted notes.

We have a plastic surgeon locally who handwrites a Thank You to every patient who sends him a referral. (A lot more impressive than a flowery computer letter.)

Considine has four different designs on fold-over double postcards and scrawls off about 1,000 a year.

You've read about the stellar cellular phone people adding clever Post-Its to existing printed material. Handwritten.

In "The Great Brain Robbery" seminars (How to steal ideas, make money and have more fun), there are converts to the importance of handwritten notes who won't leave home without 20 to 30 postcards to be sent to best customers and prospects while they sun, ski or scuba dive. It pays, they say. These cards go right on top of the mail of every executive.

Nordstrom people send handwritten notes all the time. (See "shoe story.")

Cards are cheap. Notes are quick. Makes you different . . . the impression is indelible because . . . it's personal—and—hardly anybody does it.

"Feel Good" Moves

Why not take a page out of Bag City's (San Francisco) book? Here is the insert that comes in the shipment with their leather bags:

Dear Valued Customer,
We at Bag City would like to thank you for your business

and continued support. We try very hard to sell only good quality items at a fair price. If you should experience any problems with your purchase, please call me. If we cannot repair your item, we will replace it.

[Makes you feel pretty confident so far . . .]
(The message goes on . . .)

Your checks will be deposited on the day they are dated. If you have advance knowledge of any problems, e.g., if you have closed your account or your funds are low, or if you would like to change the date on your check, please call me in advance. I will be pleased to hear from you. The alternative, a returned check, costs everybody in more ways than one.

[Here is a guy who's "been there," understands we all occasionally goof.]

Thank you once again. We look forward to serving you next time.

Sincerely yours,

(signed)
Jeffrey Maitles, Managing Director
(and gives his *personal direct* phone number.)

How far are you and your business willing to stretch to offer this kind of courtesy and thoughtfulness to your paying customers? Or do you pull back and say—"Oh we couldn't go **that** far?"

Well then, be glad you are not in direct competition with Mr. Maitles and his merry crew 'cause they'll eat you alive!

On the Other Hand . . .

For reasons beyond our belief, some businesses like to threaten customers, scold them even *before* the customer starts to do business with them.

PRIME EXAMPLE: the "welcome" sign over the entry doors of one supermarket, which shall go unnamed:

> **"All Returned Checks WILL Incur a $20 Penalty
> NO EXCEPTIONS!"**

Makes you feel warm and fuzzy, doesn't it?

Consider What Bag City Did . . .

On a one color, inexpensive card inserted with the merchandise, Bag City has covered just about all the bases any retailer (seller) should cover in creating confidence with a customer:

- thanks for your business
- we try hard to do it right
- if temporary money problems bug you, tell us
- let's avoid the totally unnecessary charges to everybody on returned checks

A slight improvement over threats, don't you think?

> QUESTION: **What customer-concerned attitude do you
> think *your* business projects?
> (Psst! Why don't you ask your customers?)**

With My Compliments . . .

He's part-time, a summer job, waiting tables at Il Fornaio, one of an impressive chain of Italian restaurants. Big guy. Football build, but charming. Great smile. Easy manner.

He hands the menu over smoothly. Gets water and drink orders without a fuss. And hallelujah! He doesn't do the "My name is _____ and I'll be your server" routine.

He mentions the specials and their prices slowly. Pauses to see if we're getting it. Asks if there are any questions, takes the order. Handles it all with aplomb. Makes just the right comments with an approving nod of his head. "Good choice! You'll like it." Any conversation is customer-started, which is how we discover he's college, part-time.

Meal's over. Check arrives, customer uses pen supplied by the big guy to sign, adds 20% tip and murmurs, "Wow, what a great pen!" lifts the pen and peers at the small writing on the barrel to read the name of the manufacturer.

"It's a Micro Ceramic," the big guy smiles."My brother's a manager at Kinko's. I get them there. I had six and now I'm down to this one." The customer scribbles on the paper placemat and repeats, "Neat pen."

"It's yours, sir, with my compliments. And thanks for coming in," and he's gone.

QUESTION: Would you hire this man for your business?

Finding the Right Ones

Really superior, brainy, heads-up people are so hard to find, executives like CEO Bob Manroe of HillCo, are taking them wherever they can find them. "Hiring by gut-feel" Bob calls it after hiring a young manager he had been watching in his San Jose health club over the period of a few months.

"The guy was always on the move," Bob said. "Great Attitude. Had that wide-awake, I-know-what's-going-on sense. Didn't miss a trick." Like what?

"Oh, he's checking if everybody has towels. He's looking around at lockers to see if they're closed. He's picking up stuff he doesn't have to pick up. He's pushing the other guys to follow up on earlier assignments. So I hired him."

QUESTION: What's he know about your business?

Manroe, laughing: "Who cares? He's got the attitude, the hustle. He didn't miss a beat in the three months I was watching him. I can teach him our business. What the hell, no sales business needs rocket scientists, just common sense and hustle. He's got it. I'm betting he'll become a manager at our place. We're growing, man. I'm gonna need people who can take charge."

That's it? You hire on pure instinct? Sometimes, you can. But remember, Bob watched the guy for three months. Plenty of time for the young man to fail. Time enough to reinforce Bob's instinct. Sure most companies will run the normal checks. Put the new recruit through the routine Company testing. Find out if the person is basically legit. (We've all been fooled at some time or other by a smooth con.) But in this crunch era of down-sizing, re-engineering, having fewer people doing more . . . where are you going to find your next "stars?"

QUESTION: Have you ever "hired on hunch" and had it work out long term?

SEISMIC CUSTOMER SERVICE

This letter was sent by Viking Business Products to California businesses immediately after a giant earthquake:

WE WANT TO HELP YOU
IF YOU NEED IT!

Everyone was affected by the earthquake.
Some of us much more than others.
If your business was damaged, we'd like to help.
Tell us what you need NOW, and we will try to do it
    NOW—at no charge.

This is NOT a sales letter. It's a sincere offer, just to help our customers. Here's a few ways we can help you, if you need it:

1. Some office supplies (no cost to you) to get you started again.
2. Replacement (free) of something you have purchased from us that was damaged in the quake.
3. Extra months to pay us for open invoices or additional purchases (no interest, no pressure—just your personal word that you'll pay).
4. Special needs—just ask us.

So, call us toll free at 1-800-421-1222 anytime. Our phone people are authorized to help you at no cost. Right now, "people and helping" are what count most. You can count on us.
Sincerely,

IRWIN HELFORD
President, Viking Business Products

Who's Paying the Bills?

IDEA: From Cary Zucker at Neutron Industries in Phoenix. Printed right on the paycheck of each employee is this:

The enclosed pay is from our customers.
It is the way they thank you for fast service,
quality products, your attention to detail,
and a caring attitude.

Signed by the President and printed in different typefaces for each week so employees will continue to take notice of it, this ought to remind them WHO IS PAYING THEIR SALARY.

NOTHING FISHY HERE!

In Miami, anxious for a top-notch seafood dinner, we put our name on a list and, knowing about the wait, waited two hours to eat at Joe's Stone Crab, a popular seafood restaurant. (Yes, we felt it was worth waiting for!)

The food and service were excellent, but more memorable was the way the owner treated us as we paid the bill: "Did everything go the way you wanted? Is there anything you can suggest to make your eating experience more pleasant?" It was the owner—not a waiter muttering, "Everything all right?"

He semi-apologized for the wait, but said their history of taking reservations was that reservations caused more problems—people didn't cancel, it was impossible to know with any accuracy how long people would stay, and he didn't want to put pressure on those dining in order to take care of those waiting. Then—did WE have any ideas on how to solve the problem of his success?

Technically you could call this "After-Sales Service" couldn't you? And this gentleman did it magnificently.

Here was a perfect example of capitalizing on a happy customer experience, asking for suggestions, and creating "future salespeople" who would recommend his restaurant when any of their friends visit Miami . . .

WHAT PRICE WINE?

A TRAVELER SPEAKS:

I was in Washington DC visiting a customer and staying at the Four Seasons Hotel in Georgetown. While having dinner at the hotel, I was perusing the wine list, looking for a bottle of wine as well as examining their wine pricing. Some restaurants and hotels mark their wine up too much and intimidate the unaware. A bottle of 1989 Chateau Meyney Bordeaux caught my eye, but was priced at $60. This wine sells for $12 to $15 at retail. With a comment about price to the sommelier I ordered something a little more reasonable.

Checking out of the hotel I was given a comment card to fill out. I decided to criticize their wine pricing strategy. I wrote that marking a bottle of wine up two or three times was sufficient and more people would probably order wine under this strategy.

About two weeks later I received a *phone call* in California from Christopher Norton, the General Manager of the Four Seasons Hotel in

Georgetown. He admitted there was a mistake on the price of that wine. They used to offer a 1982 at $60 and when they ran out they substituted the 1989. The 1982 probably justified a price of $60, he said, but certainly not the 1989 which is a recent release.

Mr. Norton informed me they were changing the price on their wine list for the 1989 to $45. I mentioned how good the service was at the hotel and how I would soon be staying at the Four Seasons in Newport Beach (California) with my wife.

Much to my surprise, when my wife and I checked into our room, two months later, at the Four Seasons in Newport Beach, sitting on the table was a bottle of 1989 Chateau Meyney! There was a note from Mr. Norton explaining that he appreciated my comments, was sorry that I had not enjoyed this wine in Georgetown, but now I could enjoy it in Newport Beach with his compliments!

Out of curiosity I checked the Newport hotel's wine list. The Chateau Meyney was not on the list in Newport Beach. This incident really showed me just how committed the Four Seasons Hotel is to Customer Service. The hotel's data bank has undoubtedly been updated cross-country with this customer's wine preference!

NOTE: After receiving this story from Mike Lamberti we were so impressed we thought about inventing a reverse slogan for WAYMISH, like WAYMISE—for Why Are You Making It So **Easy** . . . for me to give you my money! Fabulous attention to detail and then, as important, FOLLOW THROUGH.

This is certainly in line with one of Ray's seminar phrases, *Create your own Service Legends.* Four Seasons is doing it.

That Magic Touch

Your basic product or service is probably not radically different from that of your competitors. Why should the customer choose you? What makes the difference?

Research, observation and focus groups will tell you the difference . . . It's often the Intangibles. Small, surprisingly simple Intangibles.

EXAMPLE: One married couple, both avid book readers, found they were patronizing two different book stores. Why, asked the husband, when "my" book store is so close, do you travel three times further when both stores have the same books? The wife's answer: "I love the little carrot cakes they serve. That's worth the trip." Aha!

That is what we call a "Decider."
Do you think that "little carrot cakes" are listed in the Strategic Marketing Plan of the wife's book store? No way! Most of the "Deciders" are the subtle small differences that attract and keep customers but aren't "in the book," not included in the manual, aren't published as policy.

You have to seek out these subtle extras that attract and keep customers.

(Just as you have to search out their opposites: the WAYMISHes that lose customers.)

SOME TRUE STORIES

A man bought a house after weeks of looking. When asked what finally caused him to choose "this house," he answered, "The bougainvillaea bushes. I love them!" That was the Decider—unbelievable as it might seem for a $400,000 purchase.

Almost everybody we talked to prior to publishing had a personal story (an admission) of buying or patronizing a particular store/company/establishment "just because." They would tell of some seemingly minor Deciders—the attitude of a sales person, a suggestion volunteered, or a small "throw in" of an Extra at no cost, or the mere fact of being recognized, the *impression* of being recognized.

A classic example: first-time visit to a small, intimate, midtown New York City bar. The owner-maitre d' threw open his arms in welcome and, with an emotional greeting gushed, "How mah-vel-ous to see you again!" The new patron, non-plussed, stuttered, "But this is our first time here." To which Mr. Welcome instantly replied, "It doesn't matter, we are dee-lighted to have you with us! Please . . . follow me to a special place and let me introduce you to new friends." (It became our favored New York watering hole.)

Or the Memory Trick. Of all the restaurants in Harvard Square why would a returning grad always head to the Wursthaus? Because it's old Cambridge and picturesque? Maybe. But how about if Frank Cardullo, the 50-plus years proprietor, remembers what the grad drank and ordered from bygone college days!

Or, the Palm Springs car salesman who took a recently purchased car in for its first servicing, returned it with two new floor mats matching the colors of the interior (as a Thank You for buying from him) and a comment, "I noticed a small ding in the right side. I had it touched up. No charge."

Or, Murray Raphel (during his clothing days) delivering a looks-like-every-other London Fog tan trench coat; but in his, your name appears in a HUGE monogram on the inside front flap. "So you can always find your coat on a rainy day in a restaurant cloakroom."

Or, Dewey Richardson of Merit Cleaners who will put aside everything for two minutes to steam clean the just-spilled coffee spots off the tie of the harried salesman late for a morning appointment.

Or, the free cocktail or complimentary dessert at Magpie's as a make up for slow or delayed service. Or the graceful touch of delicate china cup and saucer for coffee or tea offered to gentlemen shoppers in Piscitelli's elegant clothing shoppe.

Or, the amusing clerk at Von's supermarket who whipped on an apron, went around to the long cue waiting to be checked out and whispered to the last four in line, "Quick! Follow me! I'm going to open #4 checkout"—and ran back to that cash register.

Or, Manning Press, who delivered a small order of flyers for the local Sheriff's Support Group charity event, shrugging and saying, "I printed an extra 500 in case you need them. No charge. Just sheets of paper really." (And a magic touch.)

Or, the talented designer Peter Violante whose client had a five way bypass, was out of the picture for a while, and needed artwork, type and a brochure to inform his clients where and why they hadn't heard from him. Complete camera-ready art appeared with a note: "Get well. Stay well. This one's on me. Peter."

Or, the real-estate legend of the couple teetering on the edge of decision about buying this house when the woman saw a cat rubbing its back along the baseboard of the living room. "Oh! Does the cat come with the house?" asked the woman eagerly. "Ab-so-lutely!" purred the real estate agent, crossing her fingers. The sale was closed.

Does the "Magic Touch" Work?

Of course. We could each recount examples of "touches" delivered by favorite waiters, waitresses, sales people, rental-car clerks, airline flight attendants—which convinced us, "Next time, I'm coming back here." That's a Decider and an anti-WAYMISH defense.

And as intriguing as those are, there aren't many you'd ever find in the Training Manuals—except under general headings like "Attitude"—"The customer is a Guest" and so on.

But notice, in each one of these cases above there is an element of Empowerment: the people who made the decision to give the customer "something extra" did it on their own and did it quickly. Aye, there's the secret! *On their own and did it quickly.*

And do you see any great Cost in any of these examples? No.

To repeat a prime belief of ours one more time: *The cheapest thing you can give away is . . . your own product or service.* It's an investment in the customer you already have.

You know exactly what it costs—and that's a lot less than the cost of getting a new customer or losing an old one!

Face it—the Magic Touches are like fairy dust:
hard to believe but all important to the Believers.

GREAT CATCH!

The award for Best Hotel Snafu Recovery goes to the Four Seasons Hotel in Washington DC.

Here is the comedy scene and the players are...Doorman Houston Stevens; General Manager Stan Bromle; Lisa Burns, hotel guest and PR executive; and innocent Connell Stafford, another hotel guest and Coca-Cola executive.

At 10 AM, New York PR executive Lisa Burns had her bags sent down to the front door to expedite her departure. She had to check out in a rush because of a sudden schedule change for an important client lunch in New York.

As it would happen, about the same time as Burns' bags arrive in the lobby, Connell Stafford of Coca-Cola is checking out. Doorman Stevens hails him a cab and loads the bags into the taxi. (Which bags? Uh oh!) Burns arrives two minutes later to find (or more accurately "not to find") her bags. Gone.

With no time to spare, she angrily heads to the airport. Half an hour later, Stafford arrives at Dulles and at check-in discovers he has Burns' bags. Good guy that he is, he returns to the hotel with the bags. Then, wasting no time, GM Bromley dispatches Doorman Stevens to the airport, where he hops the next shuttle flight to New York, grabs a cab and speeds to Burns' office, and beats her back from her lunch!

Now that is service above and beyond. And, for Mr. Stafford (proving his Coca-Cola manners are "the real thing"), we say Bravo!

Another Legend of Stunning Service created by Four Seasons.

COMMENDABLE COMPASSION

And certainly another special award should go to Doubletree Hotels. For years, the chain has had a nationwide community-relations program designed to provide complimentary hotel rooms for families traveling from out of town to visit loved ones receiving emergency medical treatment. Under their "Room at the Inn" program, the folks at Doubletree have already given away more than **7,600 rooms**. Wonderful.

THAT CARLYLE STYLE

"New York is full of luxury hotels but there's nothing like the fabled Carlyle—remarkably comfortable, distinctively stylish and very discreet." This and what follows are the observations of Stephen Birmingham as he describes this elegant, unbelievably client-attentive hostelry.

As the story goes, three gentlemen were in a serious business discussion in the hotel dining room. One of the guests half jokingly was overheard to say he hoped they could wind up soon because he wanted to see an episode of the TV show Twin Peaks. But it appeared the discussion would go on beyond viewing time.

As the hour of the TV show approached, an assistant manager approached and quietly said to the Peaks fan, "Excuse me, sir, I've taken the liberty of inserting a blank tape in the VCR in your room and set the timer for 10 o'clock on ABC so you can watch Twin Peaks at your leisure."

More?

Although the elevators are fully automatic, each is manned by a white-gloved operator. There are Baldwin parlor grand pianos in the larger suites since proprietor Peter Jay Sharp plays both classical and jazz piano. Because 80% of the guests are "regulars," they are not asked to produce credit cards when checking in. Checking out can be accomplished with the wave of a hand to the front desk.

Everyone is pampered to death, including the staff. During the hotel workers strike several years ago, Peter Sharp and the rest of Management brought out sandwiches and iced tea on silver trays to the picketers on the line. When it rained, they brought out umbrellas for the strikers. Now that's style. (At other hotels strikers were breaking windows.)

The ultimate? There are many . . . like the Brazilian guest who gets his daily newspaper faxed to his room from Rio. Or the guest who shipped a 50-foot yacht to the hotel asking that it be sent on to him in Texas. It was. Or when head concierge John Neary answered a call from Iceland where a **"prized Carlyle client"** was on a motor trip and low on fuel. She wanted to know where the nearest gas station would be? Mr. Neary located it for her, of course.

But the ultimate ultimate...the guest who complained to the manager she wanted an extra bedroom but didn't want to change suites. Simple. When she was out to luncheon carpenters cut a doorway into the adjacent room.

So, as you readers can see, achieving Total Customer Service is a cinch: just do absolutely positively everything and anything the customer wants. The Carlyle does it. Nothing to it.

REMEMBER ME?

Customers Do Remember

FEARGAL QUINN of Superquinn, his great Irish grocery store, is constantly checking up on his customers and customer service. He asked one of his women shoppers why she shopped Superquinn. Ahhh, the woman responded in a lilting Irish brogue. "Well, Darlin', one day I came to your wonderful checkstand with a basket heaped with food and I found I'd forgot me purse. I hid me head and told the man to hold my groceries, that I'd be right back with the money. And he smiled and said, 'Sweetheart, you're goin' nowhere. Take your groceries and pay next time you're in,' and he winked at me." Feargal was intrigued and quietly asked, "Wonderful, dear, and who was the man? Do you by any chance remember his name?" No, said the woman. And then she described him. Feargal said nothing but "Thank you, dear. See you soon!"

That man the woman remembered had not worked in Feargal's store for 14 years!

Legends of Good and Bad Service are imbedded in your mind for years and years.

THE SODA JERK

It's incredible how long a WAYMISH can be burned into the memory.

Many, many years ago, Jimmy Bernard's family patronized a local drugstore where Jimmy used to get an ice cream soda for 15 cents. (Told you it was a long time ago). One day Jimmy wanted a soda but only had a dime. So he ordered a dish of ice cream (ten cents), a large glass of ice water, and a small glass of seltzer (no charge). He drank the water, then put the ice cream and the soda in the now empty water glass and had his ice cream soda for ten cents. [Small wonder JB became a great salesman later on.]

The drugstore proprietor saw this invention, got angry and roundly scolded Jimmy and wagged his finger in Jimmy's face. All this in front of other customers. "Never try that five-cent chiseling again!"

Jimmy told his parents about being embarrassed by the owner in the drugstore. They decided as a family to take their drugstore business elsewhere. A five-cent WAYMISH? No, more . . .

Jimmy still tells this story as though it had happened yesterday. It happened in 1927.

YOU DID REMEMBER ME!

A small, cozy local restaurant had good service, comfortable ambiance, became one of those favorite Friday night, Saturday night habits. But it closed. Some financial problem.

Recently, after 18 months, it re-opened under new management. Same waiters. One of the ex-regulars decided to give the new management a try and came away astonished.

When he entered, Adolfo, the "old" waiter recognized the guest, smiled, nodded "Welcome Mr. Shackett, your usual table is ready, a Stoli with a twist is on the way."

How do these guys do that?

Recommendation for Training

"I am the Customer"—a classic Customer Service training video. In it a cordial, quiet, ordinary guy tries to do business with several local companies. The video sequences follow him from business to business and show him being stupidly hassled, not served promptly, and not recognized in a bank, although his name is clearly printed on all the checks and banking documents.

As this fictitious film customer, weary of being "dissed" (as in "dis-serviced"), gets in his car in the parking lot, he looks straight at the camera and says ever so gently, "They may not remember me or treat me like I'm important . . . but I'm the Customer and you know what? I just won't come back," and drives off.

OFF—as in GONE.

The Lifetime Value as a customer of those businesses is quietly driving away. And nobody in those businesses will ever know why.

"I am the Customer" is from **CRM Films**. An excellent 12-minute tap-on-the-face reminder like the classic skin bracer commercial that said, "I needed that!" We all do from time to time—especially for any management group or company who may *think*, "We don't need that. We are doing an excellent job of dealing with all our customers." [CRM Films can be reached at 1-800-421-0833. Tell President Peter Jordan we sent you.]

VI Ways to Keep Customers

I. **No long lines for service.** Customers hate them. The Food Marketing Institute in a national survey of women shoppers asked, "What do you want most from a supermarket." The answer was—"To get out!" [See Dick Meister "On Queue."]

II. **One informed, willing employee to assist a customer from A to Z.** Personal shoppers. Hosts. Hostesses. A Maitre d' type Welcomer (WalMart). All-around service (the Marriott door man-does-it-all concept). Or just plain, "I can help you!" attitude from all employees.

III. **Top quality value for everything your store offers.** Renowned retailer Stanley Marcus claims his father's total opposition to reducing quality during the depths of the 1930's depression set the standards for the success of famed Neiman-Marcus.

IV. **Survey and find out what people "were going to buy" and didn't.** THE KEY TO THIS IS *DON'T BE AFRAID TO ASK.* Customers love to comment—and complain. People relish being asked. For you, getting negative feedback is horrible to hear and unpleasant to face, but vital to improving your Sales! [See Lakewood Publishing story later.]

V. **Ample selection of goods.** Nordstrom has more stock, more sizes, more salespeople. You can't avoid buying if it's a question of color, style or variety. They have it. Or—will get it! [Also good idea to give staff handy pocket cards to make quick notes of customers comments. Collect and study.]

VI. **Be the First with the Most.** Trends: one youth clothing company goes out, takes candid on-the-street videos of teenagers in action to capture images of just how their future prospects play/work/live/mix and match the clothes. Then they go back and design the new lines. .

GO AHEAD—ARGUE WITH CUSTOMERS

PICTURE THIS

IT WAS ONE of those discount office supply stores. Good prices but almost every time the front-end service is horrible. Usually a comedy of errors. A glitch every visit. Wonder how they stay in business?

Here's the latest: Wife wants to purchase a chart pad and a picture frame. No UPC code on the frame so the cashier begins searching for price in a catalog. Check-out phone rings. Cashier stops everything to answer the phone. Customer waits while cashier is engaged in telephone conversation. Maddening.

Finally . . . cashier is ready to resume transaction. Wife informs cashier she has in the meantime checked the price: "The frame's on sale at $2.99."

Cashier doesn't listen, doesn't respond to customer, starts rifling through a price catalog and finds "something similar" to the frame and announces in a triumphant tone: "No, the price is $7.95!"

That's the way to go . . . Insult the Customer. Question her honesty. And above all, don't be polite and ask the Customer where she found the sale price . . . No, irritate the Customer. (Who trained this idiot?)

Now the Customer is mad enough that she tells the cashier, "Forget it!"—she doesn't want the frame, just the chart pad.

Cashier, without a mutter, sets the frame aside and completes the transaction for only the chart pad, takes the money, end of story.

Where did the cashier go wrong? Let's step through it:

(1) She neglected a customer in the middle of a sale for the telephone call. She should have explained to whoever called her, she was ringing up sales and taking care of her customer —first, especially if the customer is ready and waiting to pay **money** . . . WAYMISH.

(2) Nor did she bother to be polite and re-check the frame price against the customer's information. At a minimum, all clerks should know or have access to in-store specials.

(3) Management's fault to allow incoming calls to check-out positions . . . or at least to **train** cashiers on how to handle the conflicts of cash customer versus phone caller.

(4) Losing a sale, no matter how small, without a comment, apology or attempt to recapture the sale is really poor! That says *we don't want the business. Take it or leave it. Makes no difference to me.*

BIG difference! $5 was the difference in cost of the frames. What is the cost of the Lost Customer . . . in *"future dollars?"* Hundreds, or over the next five to ten years, thousands. Scary.

Moral: Think *Long Term*.

P.S. [Poor Selling]

Questions on discarded items from an experienced retailer:

1. How do you follow-up on those items set aside in your checkstands?
2. Do you ask why they were discarded?
   (Was it: not enough money to cover the total purchase price? An argument over price? Customer changed her mind?)
3. Find out what *other* reasons shoppers gave for discarding intended purchases.

Each answer can supply good marketing information.

Ask the People Who Deal with the Customer

Probing, without beating up your check-out and delivery people, can give you a great deal of valuable information, including ideas for improved Customer Service and suggest new directions for increasing sales.

LET'S SHARE, SHALL WE?

A well-to-do couple who eat out regularly and patronize this mid-scale fish specialty restaurant chose it once again for an evening's meal.

She was hungry. He wasn't. She ordered a full size fish salad knowing from past experiences the portions were more than generous. He ordered a bowl of soup, planned to eat some rolls and have iced tea.

As dinner progressed, she frowned and said, "I can't eat all this; here, take that butter plate and take some of mine." He did. As the waiter passed, he scanned the table, stopped and in a scolding tone announced: "I'll have to charge you $4 extra because you're splitting portions!"

The Other Half

Enroll your collection and accounts receivable people on the anti-WAYMISH team. They don't get to see customers. So search for problems and suggest ways that won't alienate and drive customers to your competitors. Make it possible for the slower payer to save face. Find out specifically why a closed account went elsewhere. Hold customer-retention meetings. Write down problems. Look for trends. Resolve the problem. Talk Lifetime Value of Customer—not "Collecting the Last Dollar Due." It might cost too much.

ONE HAND DOESN'T KNOW
WHAT THE OTHER—

Bergdorf-Goodman has been Big Time in retailing forever. So when the other famous names got into catalogs and mail order, naturally Bergdorf joined the game. During the usual Christmas toll-free 800 number shopping spree, repeated calls were made to Bergdorf on a weekend to order articles de femme, clothes for the ladies of the family. "Repeated" because the call-us-anytime lines were busy, busy, busy. On the weekend? Okay. Good! They must be doing business!

Many busy signals later, finally—Hooray!—a human contact.

The catalog companies have long ago trained their operators to first ask "Name/Address/Zip" and "the credit card you plan to use?" *before* they will allow you to state the item you want to order.

Weary and wily veteran catalog shoppers do not respond to this routine trap question. The accomplished shopper interrupts gently and says, "Let me ask you a question: Is this item available? I would like to know that first." The good companies answer immediately.

The Bergdorf "call-us-anytime-ready-to-serve-you" reply: "Oh, to find that out, you'll have to call a different number Monday—"

What? This is Saturday. What happened to the 24 hour "our-operators-are-standing-by" pitch? And, in this day of instant computer databases, incoming order takers have no way of knowing whether the item is in stock? **What is this?**

And call another number? Forget it! Good-bye Bergdorf. Hang up. I've got 16 other color-filled catalogs stacked from last week's "Shop with us for Christmas!" mail.

Lost sale for Bergdorf and a Bad Impression—and more. Read on!

The P.S. to this true story is the caller dialed the Horchow catalog in Dallas. As soon as their mail order lady came on the line she said, "If you would give me your telephone number, sir, I can save you a lot of time on this call." (Yea! Someone who has leaped over the WAYMISH wall!)

Eager-to-buy Caller gives phone number. "Mr. Considine, 1029 North Allen, Pasadena?" she gently purrs. "Yeah," says the caller surprised at the nano-second response, "How do you do that?" "From your telephone number, sir . . . "

Does Roger Horchow have the entire WORLD on his computer? Very impressive. And Yes, the caller ordered—several fairly expensive items. (Damn the cost, it's Christmas and these Horchow people really know what they're doing!)

Suggestion: Bergdorf . . . Call Roger Horchow for his tips on How To Make It Easier for the Customer to do business with you . . . It's called getting rid of the WAYMISH. Roger's number is . . . 1-800-395-5397.

FedEx's customer-sensitive system identifies you from your incoming call. No one has to ask even your phone number.

Question for any company with a phone ordering service:

How much money are you wasting for the time you pay your service people?

Why are they taking down all that lengthy, useless pre-ordering information—name/address/zip/phone/credit card—only to find out (a) you don't have the item, (b) can't close the order or (c) can't get any money back for all the information you paid to accumulate when there was *no order*?

A heads-up salesman we know—John Sheehan—says, "Fish where the fish are. Ain't no fish, why spend for the boat, the line, the bait and the hook?"

LET'S HAVE A DRINK . . .

Three perky, ready-to-have-fun ladies dropped into Houlihan's Bar in Boston and purposely picked an open table right next to the bar to get a better table and faster service. The place was 70% empty. A WAYMISH waitress came over: "You can't sit here. It's reserved in case of a late rush. You'll have to move."

The three startled women looked around. Rush? What rush? The three were all ex-waitresses, and one had been a bartender. "This is ridiculous!" snapped one. "This place looks like an empty barn!" They refused to move. Houlihan's finest walked away.

The leader of the frustrated ready-to-spend trio went up to the hostess and complained: "We want to get some appetizers and some drinks. We want to sit near the bar. And that waitress won't serve us."

The WAYMISH hostess replied in a superior tone,,"That's up to her. That's her station. If she doesn't want to serve you, she doesn't have to do it." Whaaat? The ladies noisily grabbed their purses, stormed out and yes—did write a seething letter to the manager, who in turn sent them an abject apology offering free dinners for all three.

I wonder—did they bother to go back for their free dinners? And if they did—was the same wonderful WAYMISH waitress there?

Who "owns" the business—the servers?
Who makes the rules for the asylum—the inmates?

GROUNDED FLYERS

Dan Pappalardo is a computer/video whiz who lives with and loves images and design. He visits the opening of an art gallery and spots on the counter a stack of beautifully printed full-color flyers featuring the gallery show items. So he politely asks, "May I have one?" reaching his hand out and expecting an automatic cordial, "Of course!"

An emphatic, "NO!" jolts him. "These are only for our clients," snaps the dim-witted guardian of the flyers as she makes a motion to gather them in and protect them like her young.

A woman next to Dan laughed, "How do they get **new** clients?" and walked off. Dan smiled, turned back to the flyer-retentive attendant and asked, "Well . . . how **do** you get new clients?"

"Whaddaya mean?" was the brilliant retort. [Good question.]

****

Quick thought: If you give part-time help or volunteers a temporary assignment, be sure somebody makes clear that their main responsibility is to sell . . . whether that means just being nice to customers, helpful to prospects, or giving out information freely—happily!
Is there any one in your company who feels he has to
"guard the pamphlets"
and prevent their distribution at all costs?

Compadre Murray Raphel has a parallel gem of a story. On a shopping visit to a supermarket for which his company had created a series of full-color selling brochures Murray, ever watchful and observant, asked the owner curiously, "Hi . . . by the way, where are the brochures we designed for you? I thought they looked *great*!"

"Oh yeah, they're great," mutters the owner opening a drawer, and pointing inside it, "but I keep them in here."

"Wh-Wh-Why?" stammers Murray.

"Because they cost 25 cents a piece and people kept taking them!"

Well, that's one way to keep promotion costs down.

TEMPER, TEMPER....

1. Speaker was asked to call a company sponsoring a large national conference. Evidently the people answering were hired guns handling inquiries and reservations for the meeting. The caller asked for Mr. Jim Rhode, president of the sponsoring company. Seemed simple . . .

The abrasive reply: "WE run the conference. There's no Jim Rhode here!" Jim Rhode is a very pleasant, low-key man, smooth professional. It would kill him to hear that anybody treated any of his prospects like that. There's that Front Line, at it again. But who knows what they're doing? (Later the speaker was personally treated exceptionally well by the Rhodes.)

2. Lady had her BMW in for full service, lubrication, grease and oil, check the hoses, the whole ball of wax—and a nice profit for this so-called service station. The car was up on the lift and was finished.

After the mechanic lowered the car, the customer rather timidly asked, "Could you check the muffler? I thought it sounded loose . . . or something."

The mechanic scowls at her in disgust and snarls, "Jeez, lady! Why didn't you tell me that when I had the car up on the lift?"

The mechanic re-trained would say, "Sure," smile, give a twist of the wrist to reverse the hydraulic lift, have a look, and make . . . maybe some more profit?

3. Man received a Christmas gift certificate good for $50 at a local CD-record store. He knew what selections he wanted, knew where those CDs were stocked. He went and checked the prices (which came to within 15 cents of his $50 gift), scooped up the CD packages, took them to the counter, laid the certificate on the counter, told the clerk he didn't care about the insignificant difference between the $49.85 and the $50 and could he just take the CDs and leave?

Easy sale, right? No. This WAYMISH wonder snapped, "Why dontcha come in some time when you're not in such a hurry!"

Slowly, the avid CD collector picked up his CDs and departed—permanently.

Could have been an easy sale, right? But who's watching the store or checking the counter?

WAYMISHes like this happen much too often. And there is no way you can know what your customer contact people are doing (at any level) unless you or an MBWA (Management By Walking Around) manager are "out there."

Another option would be to encourage what we now call **TOA—Train One Another.**

This is an interesting, mature, "intra-team" training concept. TOA encourages peers, fellow clerks and managers, any employees who are on the same level, to coach each other. That way, everyone is coaching on a very informal level.

EXAMPLE: With our thoughtless garage "lift engineer," after the lady leaves, another mechanic shouts over: "Hey—that customer was all right. Why get on her case? What's eating you today?"

TOA certainly works on a professional sports level. Players earning millions of dollars a season will be pointing, directing, instructing team mates where to move, how to "make the play." And when it's success-ful, watch the high five's, the chest bumping and thumbs up. It's not criticism, it's team work—and you can generate the same excitement when your staff becomes a TOA Service TEAM.

TO BALANCE OUT THE "WRONGS"...

Here are three "Rights" (from *Consumer Reports,* Dec. 95)

One—When a Michigan reader informed North Face the zipper on his parka had lost its zip (after several years), North Face sent him a new parka.

Two—A Virginia reader's Trane heat pump went haywire. After three years, it needed a new circuit board. The customer paid for the repairs, but curious about it, asked Trane what might have gone wrong. Although the pump was under warranty for one year, Trane sent an apology and a check to cover the cost of the repaired part.

Three—Forty years after receiving a Cross pencil as a high school graduation present, a man sends the non-working pencil back to Cross. Three days later a new pencil arrives—with an apology.

LESSON: **It's in the details. People paying attention get the cus-tomer's attention—and loyalty.**

Bonus

We'd like to add a bonus from *Front Line Customer Service* by Clay Carr, published by John Wiley & Sons, which echoes our sentiments (except for the use of "him" to describe all customers.)

1. From the point of view of your customers (potential, actual, or former), your only excuse for being in business is to satisfy them.
2. You don't sell products or service or even benefits. You sell value—or you don't sell anything at all!
3. Customers define value in their own terms. If you want to satisfy them, you have to look at your products or services through their eyes—always!
4. If anything happens after the sale to prevent the customer from getting at least the value he expected, he hasn't gotten the value he paid for—and the customer knows it! In short, you've created a dissatisfied customer.
5. Dissatisfied customers aren't problems; they're golden opportunities.
6. The really picky, demanding customers are platinum opportunities. Keep satisfying them, and you're in business for life.
7. If you intend to deal successfully with dissatisfied customers, focus on saving the customer, not on saving the sale. [We heartily agree.]
8. Either customer satisfaction and loyalty are primary, or something else is. No compromise is possible.
9. Your frontline people won't treat your customers any better than you treat your frontline people.
10. When a customer provides honest comments, he's doing you a favor—and that's how he looks at it. Give him a reason to do you the favor.
11. To satisfy an unhappy customer, you must add extra value to make up for the value you promised but failed to provide in the first place.

12. Always treat a customer as if he will remain a customer. Never treat him as though this is the last time you'll see him. ["Customers for Life!" should be your credo.]

13. Always provide a dissatisfied customer a positive reason for dealing with you again.

14. The whole process by which you create and deliver your product or service must support the creation of customer satisfaction and loyalty.

15. Every organization has customers—every one. The organizations that thrive and prosper and feel good about what they do are those that consistently satisfy their customers.

AMEN.

STYMIED BY THE SYSTEM

STOP THE PRESSES! (MAYBE)

CALLED THE *New York Times* with this request: stop city delivery for several weekends, stop all delivery at the end of the month, and start a mail service to Maine. The person answering the 800 number said that she couldn't handle the first two requests on the same day. Why not? The two orders would cancel each other!

Finally convinced her to make the second change herself without requiring me to make another call.

As for the mail order to Maine, she couldn't handle that—it was a different phone number and required a separate call. WAYMISH: Why do they make it so hard to do business with them?

Is a supervisor monitoring calls?

Who are the telephone sales trainers?

More basic—*who designed the system?* The problem is not the person taking the phone call. *It's the management that never tested the process.*

E.T. (Executive At Top)
Call home! You have a problem!

RURAL RUNAROUND

My husband ordered home delivery of our local newspaper. Because we live in a rural area where no street numbers are used, I was concerned that the carrier would have trouble finding us. Sure enough, we missed deliveries several days despite frequent calls to the circulation department. Finally I phoned to cancel the subscription. "You'll have to tell me your exact location," the woman on the line said, "we can't cancel the subscription unless we know where you live."

WHO'S IN LINE?

Meanwhile, at . . .
Bank of New York, Madison Avenue and 73rd Street
Time: 3:30 PM
Situation: Eleven customers are waiting in line.
Starting time of standing in line is 3:32.
Two out of four tellers are closed, "proving" their work in order to balance out their accounts for the day. (It's now 3:37 PM.)
Irritating observation: Signs at the tellers' windows say: "You are my top priority." Really . . . Me? Gee . . . .
After what seems like an interminable wait (it is now 3:43), the customer finally gets served and then strides over to ask the bank officer at the nearest desk, "How can I be your top or first priority (pointing to the sign) when two of your four tellers are not serving customers?"
He looks up and answers coolly, "They have to prove their daily work."
Customer: "Why don't the tellers prove their work after the bank closes at 4:00 PM, on their time, not mine?"
No answer from the bank officer. Amazing.

WHAT IF the unhappy bank customer waiting in line is one of those legendary millionaires who, in a fit of pique, would next day cancel ALL his accounts and name the disinterested officer as the reason. A head would roll. Stammered excuses would flow, "But I didn't know who this customer was—I . . . "
Shouting. Scolding. Heavy account losses. Pandemonium in the money place.

Truth: No one these days can tell me how important any customer is.

Thomas Hoving of New York's Metropolitan Museum of Art tells of being very busy and being bothered by a little old lady who insisted on a personal museum tour. Begrudgingly, but politely, he conducted a tour. As the tour ended the lady commented, "This lobby certainly needs improving." Mr. Hoving agreed, "Yes, but that would cost about six million dollars."

The next morning a check arrived from the little lady for 10 million dollars. She had decided six wouldn't do it.

And by the way, she later sent a check for another million dollars so there would be fresh flowers every day. She was Lila Acheson Wallace, a co-founder of the *Readers Digest*. Nice.

SMALL CHANGE

Legend has it . . .

Sun-tanned dude walks into southwestern bank. Cashes check, exits, returns, smiles. "Forgot to get my parking ticket validated."

Super-intelligent teller: "Sorry, sir . . . cashing a check doesn't qualify as a transaction. You'll have to pay 75 cents for parking."

"Fine," says the dude evenly. "Here's your 75 cents. Now kindly withdraw the million and a half dollars in my accounts so I can take it to the bank across the street. . . ."

PIN, PIN, WHO'S HIDING THE PIN?

Debbie takes the family Jeep in for service. Service man told her he couldn't check out or repair the Jeep without the PIN number. Do you have your PIN number?

"What is a PIN number?" she asks, trying to be polite.

"The vehicle identification number stamped on the engine."

Well, shoot, we all know those numbers by heart, don't we? Once a week, we all go out, lift the hood and check the numbers on our engine block, just to make sure we still have the right automobile. And so what if the PIN number is a dyslexic combination of numbers and letters 18 to 19 characters long? We customers should know it by heart, right?

Feeling like the victim of a star chamber inquisition, Debbie fired back a question: "Why doesn't this Jeep agency have a record of the PIN ID? We bought this Jeep here!" Rag-wiper shakes his head in a series of silent No's.

Anger-motivated, Debbie snapped, "You mean there is no way you can identify this Jeep by owner name, license plate, customer record or something other than the PIN Number on the block?"

No positive response yet. So she zaps him with this one: "How about *you* opening the hood and checking the engine block, chum?" Hell hath no fury like a Jeep owner scorned.

With the marks this guy was scoring in Customer Alertness, it's surprising he didn't hand Debbie the magic mechanic's rag and ask her to open the hood and search for the PIN.

We all know the Service Departments in our businesses are not responsible for Sales.

_____TRUE   _____FALSE

THE BIGGER THEY ARE...

. . . the tougher it is to get everybody, all the way down the line, to pay attention to the corporate Mission Statements on Customer Service.

What's bigger than AT&T? Who's generally better on Service?

STORY: Lambda Chi Alpha fraternity at the University of Southern California. AT&T announces a smart heads-up multiple phone card promotion: Sign up your fraternity brothers and AT&T pays the fraternity a buck a piece. Mike Kelley, the Irish super salesman in the Lambda Chi house, signs up 148 Lambdas.

In the fraternity's newsletter, Kelley announces, "We earned a total of $148 since the brotherhood sold 148 cards." And then adds,

"However, those bastards at AT&T never sent us the money." And continued, "But the promotion accomplished two things. It brought the membership of the house closer together, and it was the last time I did any business with AT&T." The killer ending of his published report: "To this day I have an MCI calling card." And this newsletter goes out to the entire Southern California membership of Lambda Chi!

A smart affinity promotion. A new customer shoo-in . . . turned to shambles because somewhere in the Big Organization someone didn't pay attention to a small $148 detail.

Never mind how far this WAYMISH damage spread through the layers of loyal Lambda Chi alumni newsletter readers. The saddest news is: the offender will never be traceable.

NO VAT. AND THAT'S THAT

When Tony Pompeo heard the title of this book would be "WAYMISH (Why Are You Making It So Hard For Me To Give You My Money)," he snapped his fingers and said, "Listen to this! You won't believe it."

Tony talks: "When I bought my "Beemer" (BMW) in Munich, I naturally planned to register it in Italy where I was stationed at the time with AT&T. I totally underestimated the resistance of the bureaucracy in Italy."

From the BMW factory in Germany, he drove the new car to Milan, went to the Italian Registry, equivalent to the DMV in the States, and tried to register the car. WAYMISH Bureaucrat Numero Uno immediately handed the factory registration papers back to Tony and snapped, "These must be translated from German to Italian!"

Tony figured no problem, he'd go to the Italian dealership in Milan, get their handy-dandy already-printed version of BMW papers and PREGO. FINITO!!!

He did that. And with the Italian dealer version in hand, he returned in minor triumph only to have bureaucrat #2 sneer, "Oh no!

Not acceptable. This cannot be from a dealer. This has to be an official **factory** translation."

INFORMATION: There is a nasty thing in Europe called VAT—Value Added Tax—the tab you pay for bringing anything into a country which was bought elsewhere. But being of a mind to be a good citizen, do the right thing, etc. . . . Tony felt this constant rebuffing of his attempts to give the Italian Government his (their) money was really getting tiresome, and tempting him to by-pass the Italian VAT registration process.

"My company territory was all Europe," he continues, "and then someone suggested that the next time I go to Holland, why not register the car there? The Dutch are much more business-like and sensible." And in Amsterdam the Dutch lived up to their "let's do business" reputation. In, out, zip, zap, car registered; even got tourist plates on the Beemer with an "NL" or Nederlands identity badge to boot. And this Dutch identity gave Tony great privilege: he could park just about anywhere in Italy, Switzerland or Holland.

So although he tried many times to pay VAT to his temporarily adopted Italy—some multi-millions of Lira (about $10,000)—the bureaucracy for more than 15 weeks repeatedly (and successfully?) totally blocked him from giving them his (their) money. Terrific. Small wonder some governments operate at a deficit.

Tony swears if he ever got the chance to talk to an Italian government official, now that he is out of the country, he would tell this story and then ask: "Perche mi fai tante difficolta per darti I miei soldi!" (Why Are You Making It So Hard . . . for me to give you my Lira?)

Let's Play Telephone Tag . . . (and you'll never ever reach me! . . . Ha! Ha!)

Voice Mail as a concept is divided into two camps. Those in favor **(For)** are accountants, chief financial officers, corporate cost-cutters. Those not in favor **(Against)** are we **Customers** who call in trying to give you our money. Basically, we are anxious to talk to a human being, and we're not thrilled with being forced to go through interminable labyrinths of electronic messages. One favorite is, "If you know the extension of the person you're calling . . . " How the hell as an outsider do I know *extensions*—unless your people are telling me, publicizing extensions, or printing them on their business cards and faxes. Very few are.

And we customers love the "press this, press that" instructions. Love it just as much as the phone bills we're running up helplessly listening to your Telephone Tag Game. Our personal rule: We hear the phrase "Voice Mail . . . " Zap! We punch "0" for Operator as fast as Wyatt Earp could draw and fire! Even that doesn't work universally.

WARNING: Voice Mail can be dangerous to the health of your business . . . regardless of its convenience to you and as cost-cutting as it may be for the payroll. At minimum . . . have someone outside your company, friendly to you but objective . . . check out your Voice Mail for frustrating WAYMISHes. Falling victim to the Curse of Assumption (Everything's OK) can cost you Big Bux.

TICKETS, PLEASE

Theatre Playhouse Phone Message (taped and transcribed):

You have reached the ticket services department. Exact seating can not be given out over the phone. (Uh oh.) Have a credit card ready. (Yes sir!) Press "0" now for tickets. For general information stay on the line. Press "0" for the general operator (live). Stay on for anything else, if you don't have a touch-tone phone. (I'm getting confused . . .) Now accepting subscription orders . . . Press 3 for subscription information. Tickets available for . . . Press 4 for more information. Press 5 for parking and directions. Press "0" for other information from ticket service department. For information not from ticket service department, press 6 for the administration office. They are open from 10 to 6. Press the extension for the party you wish to reach. Press 9 for a directory of extensions.

And all we wanted to do was buy tickets for live theatre and we got robot rejection.

Our top Unfavorite taped message from that same theatre (even if you do get to the correct extension): "You've reached the right extension at the wrong time!" The wrong time?

Excuse me . . . I called you. Why are you telling me this is the "wrong time?" For whom, you? Or are you blaming me for trying to contact you?   How rude.

Well, we like to support live theater but maybe we'll go to the movies instead, or just rent a video.

MAKING IT EASY
TO DO
BUSINESS WITH ME

W HOLESALE DRUG FIRMS in Northern New Jersey typically sent a truck to retail stores—even on a $50 order (with a 22% gross profit).

One thinking wholesaler asked himself whether he could come up with a different plan that would combat the lazy retailers' lack of planning yet save him, the wholesaler, delivery costs.

Here's his elegant solution. "Mr. Retailer, you can PLACE your orders any time, any day, but we will DELIVER to you only once a week, during the same scheduled two-hour period so your people can be available to handle the goods. In exchange for giving up the old system, we'll cut OUR prices four percent."

He made it EASY to do business with him!—on his terms.

Four rules for market-customer-focused management

We like the crux of this article from the *Harvard Business Review* January-February 1994: **"A Day with the Customer."**

l. Recognize that the customer means more than the next step in a distribution chain.

Don't think of your marketplace offering as a *commodity.* Enthusiastic references from your satisfied customers may be the best source of new business.

CASE: An organization called every client who left them to find out why they left. Six months later they called those same ex-clients to see if they would consider returning. Five to ten percent did!

2. Count on your customers for information.

But DON'T count on them for insights. They can share their experiences and their needs, but you have to solve their problems and interpret what they are really saying.

CASE: A company selling water treatment chemicals found out over time that their commercial customers liked the chemicals but didn't like being involved in the treatment process. Gradually the company selling the chemicals took over the treatment side of the business. Customers were freed up to concentrate on their core business. Please note: The customers never asked for the service, but the company read the market correctly.

The chemical company followed this profitable marketing course: *Find more products—and services—to sell to your present customers, rather than finding new customers to sell your products to.*

3. Find out what your salespeople do.

And find out what your customers actually want from your salespeople.

CASE: A lumber company survey found that major customers didn't want salespeople calling them unless they had something new in hand—equipment, an innovative financing plan, faster delivery or a way of handling excess inventory. They also found it was the small customers who often needed more guidance and personal visits. With most of their larger customers, order-taking by phone was fine and saved the buyers time.

Caution: Don't be disappointed if customer studies don't come up with a rocket scientist's insights. Small improvements in your operations can emerge from the market-customer viewpoint—extra touches that make it easier to do business with you—faster ordering, quicker fulfillment, simpler forms, being cheaper and more fun (Southwest Airlines), express payment. Each can add up to significant improvement in customer satisfaction.

CASE: A mechanical contractor distributed his strong financial balance sheet. This made it easier for his customers to get bonding and also gave them confidence that he'd be in business to finish the job. He sent out his accurate invoices quickly and made it easier for general contractors to get paid.

4. Don't depend on just Sales to tell you what customers want.

Meet and talk to your customers at management levels. (MBWA again.) Involve all levels of your organization in your drive to be market- and customer-focused.

CASE: The Hill Companies, the largest insulation and fireplace company in the west, invites their customer-buyers to their annual meetings. In candid panel discussions called "The Firing Line" Hill asks, "How Can We Do More Business with You? Translation: *what-does-the-customer-want.* "The trick is," says President Bob Manroe, "first to get the customers' ideas, then to follow through, make the changes in our system and drive those changes down through the entire organization. That's what takes time. Hearing the ideas is the easy part."

The Way It Is

A WAYMISH is often described as a system failure. Our opinion is that most system failures are *not* failures at all. They're a basic part of management's design, the way it "works best" for Operations, Inventory, Cost Accounting, or some other company division. Not the customer.

For example, you want to buy an all-cotton sweater to be worn under a sports jacket. The sweaters in the specialty store are stacked on counters by size, but not by materials. You search through the piles, find one you like, try it on and then look for the cashier, where you wait in line.

If you don't find a sweater that suits you, you've got to find a knowledgeable person (a good trick) and place a special order. If you want the sweater wrapped, you have to go to another line and pay extra.

This is a typical barrier-to-buying WAYMISH experience. The system of stocking satisfies the operational people of the store but is frustrating, time-consuming and aggravating to the customer. Doesn't the store want to make it *easy* for the customer to spend his/her money?

But it's not a mistake or a failure. It is exactly what the store's management intends you to experience. Why? Because they assume that a system which reduces human interaction is less likely to go wrong, is cost-saving, and requires minimum-wage people who don't have to know much and offer only minimal service.

This industrial model of the consumer business world where systems and technology predominate and human contact is minimized is almost guaranteed to turn off customers.

And it does.

[Warren Bennis, the Leadership guru (and friend) from University of Southern California predicts: The manufacturing plant of the future will have only two employees—a man and a dog. The man to feed the dog and the dog to keep the man from touching the machinery.]

Except for ATM machines, which people find convenient because they're available twenty-four hours a day, most reductions of human service are negative. (One wag suggested banks run ads saying: "Our ATM's are friendlier than our tellers." And faster, too!)

Reducing service in restaurants, hotels, hospitals, gas stations and department stores has multiplied customer dissatisfaction. But that will change. Personal-service, customer-focused entrepreneurs will bite away pieces of these automated markets.

> Prediction. . . at the end of every automated market
> is the beginning of a new market—personal services.

Why are so many people buying from catalogs?

Is it because no one in retail stores is available to *take our money?* What a hassle . . . But there is rarely a hassle with catalog operations. Satisfaction is guaranteed—from the "You be the Judge" guarantee of Eddie Bauer, to Land's End, to the legendary L.L. Bean service. The catalog telephone people are generally marvelous. They take care of the WAYMISHes—without question. And learn from them.

WAYMISHes erupt when we are forced to talk to the computer, voice mail and answering machines. That makes a lot of us go ballistic. Frustration triggers an immediate desire to find "somewhere else" to buy and spend our money!

Give us *people* **to talk to!** We're reasonable. We don't want the world. We want to hear some *live person* say nicely, "Glad to help. Just tell me what you want, please."

IF YOU THINK YOU'RE SAVING MONEY
with low-cost operations, semi-trained
staff and part-time people,
we hope you'll be around for
the next ten years.

A Thought From Japan

KAIZEN: *The Art of Constant Small Improvements.*

1. Attack problems a little bit at a time: incremental improvements. This is how Honda works to make their cars better. They don't wait for model year changes, or a new operations manual or the Board of Directors. They improve each batch of cars as improvements are developed.

2. Why is this approach better than a grand design?
   People are busy doing their work; useful small changes can be implemented quickly, tested, digested, spread—with minimum disruption, risk and threats. Small constant changes breed a comfortable environment of change and experimentation and confidence.

3. It's Learn by Doing—not waiting for a detailed plan.
4. It's also called Ready–Fire–Aim. Forget the slow research process. Try it! See if it works. If it doesn't work, Stop. Now you know that it didn't work.
5. But . . . WHAT IF IT DOES WORK? Aha! Progress. A small step, and better than yesterday. Each day a small step.

---

8 WAYS TO
HIGH LEVEL CUSTOMER SATISFACTION

1.
Your strategic plan puts customer satisfaction first.

2.
The plan is not a secret. Tell everyone your goals.

3.
Highlight your goals in meeting agendas, lunchroom
signs, and in publicized rewards, promotions.

4.
Measure customer satisfaction daily by establishing
performance standards. Let those responsible for
customer contact know how they're doing.

5.
Hire people who like people!

6.
Educate people from the time they're hired.
Prove you think they're important

7.
Create an environment that encourages employees to
pursue customer satisfaction.

8.
Treat your employees as you would treat valuable customers.

EMPOWERED TO DO WHAT

THIS IS HOW IT'S DONE

U NHAPPY GUEST, an attorney, shows a San Francisco hotel desk clerk a laundry box: "You scorched and ruined my shirt!" Clerk did not ask to open box, he simply requested the guest's name and asked how much the shirt cost. The guest shrugged and "guessed about $25." Apologizing to the guest, the front desk man informed the cashier to immediately credit the guest's account for $25. "Will there be anything else, sir?"

REPORT: One WAYMISH. One complaint. One instant Make Good. One important customer saved. One small service legend created. One more story told all around Los Angeles.

READ THE SIGN!

SCENE: A Mexican Restaurant (Vail, Colorado).
SIGN: "Wait to be seated."
Several servers whooshing by announce to a waiting party of six: "The hostess will be with you in a moment." The restaurant was 90% empty.

QUESTION: Why couldn't one of the passing waiters/waitresses seat these patrons? What happened to Empowerment? Is there some highly-skilled talent required to pick up six menus, and walk to an empty table?

REACTION: Six ready-to-eat, ready-to-spend customers walked out.

RESULT: No sale. Plus, more trouble because every one of these six people (by proven research) will tell at least 11 other people: "Don't go to that restaurant! The service is lousy." Each WAYMISH multiplies into major lost revenue long term.

Forget the restaurant . . .
Does every one of your employees—at every level—**know**, and have they **been instructed** on how they must greet, direct, serve, assist **any**body who enters or contacts your business?
(Are you sure?)

YOU'RE ASKING *ME* TO MAKE AN EXCEPTION?

Daughter Karen shopping at local supermarket, Westchester County, New York.

Over the checkout counters in this busy suburban market are a bewildering array of signs: "5 or fewer items, 10 or fewer items, 15 or fewer items, More than 15 items." (Manager must have a dominant accounting gene.)

Karen had 17 items, and there were long lines at the "More than 15," but no one at the "15 or fewer." So she took a chance and hopped over to the check-out associate at the "15 or fewer."

"Could you please check me out even though I have 17 items?" (A reasonable request, wouldn't you say, since no one was there.)

The clerk pauses, apparently in deep thought (probably contemplating Einstein's Theory of Numerical Relativity), then with a sigh, grudgingly grunts, "Oh, I guess so."

How about: "Sure! Glad to! Nobody else here at the moment. Let's go!" And why not? By the time he rings up two items (seven seconds), his check-out count is down to "15 or fewer" and he has created a happy customer.

QUESTION: **Are your people empowered and willing to make** *small common sense exceptions?*

Might be worth checking it out in person, Managers. Appear and take a look.

Use your degree of MBWA = Management By Walking Around. It is the surest way to get information other than by carefully shrouded statistical reports. See for yourself.

LATE SNACK

Man's coming home late, stops at a decent semi-fast food sit-down restaurant for a cup of coffee and some pie. Missed dinner. Goes toward the podium. Man raises a finger to the Table Seater Guy as silent signal for "one" and quietly adds, "I'd like to eat and run if you don't mind."

Table Seater Guy is on automatic pilot: "Be a minute sir, have a seat." Man looks around. One family of four waiting. No one else. He waits. Then notices that behind the Table Seater podium are two tables with empty cups, scattered dirty silver and crunched up napkins.

Man says, "How about those two tables for us?" motioning to include the foursome.

"They have to be cleared," says Robot Table Seater.

Man: "How about you cleaning them?"

Icy retort: "I have to stay here to seat people," he says with an arched eyebrow.

Man: "There's nobody to seat except us."

Pure hate emanates from this guy's eyes and then he turns away and ignores everybody.

Waiting unnecessarily is a dangerous WAYMISH. Indifference on the part of employees accounts for 68% of lost customers.

"Walkouts" are a total loss. You've paid all the upfront expenses—building, promotion, signs, staff, inventory . . .

Why have customers come ready to buy . . . and then not have the employees ready to respond (trained) to accommodate reasonable customer requests?

Or worse—be ignored?

Every one of your employees should be trained, instructed and empowered to "take care of it"—whatever "it" is—especially if they are anywhere near the problem to be solved. Regardless of their title or other duties.

Question: do you have **working managers . . .** or, **"I-Don't-Do-That" managers?**

Surrounded

Isn't it a thrill to be in a restaurant where every server who passes your table quickly checks, reacts, removes dishes, serves water, pours coffee, responds to any signal you give?

In any situation where you're ready to buy and every clerk/sales person/waiter you see or talk to helps you and makes it easy for you to spend your money, all sides are happier. Everybody's having a good time!

Balducci's restaurant in San Fernando Valley (Los Angeles) surrounds you with Service. McCormick & Schmick's will do anything for you, including turning down the music or changing the music tape. Walking through the Puritan Clothing Store in Falmouth, Mass. is like going to a Tony Robbins motivational seminar!

How about finding one of these UP establishments and taking your key people there to SEE IT—PROVE TO THEM—there are regular businesses out there that make spending money with them Fun!

THE WRONG WAY AND
MRS. ROBALEDO

We hired a young lady who just two days ago had moved to California from Chicago. She is studying drama, will work for us part time and was to report to work today, but . . . She had hurriedly written down her phone number on her resume yesterday as she left. She failed to appear this morning. We were concerned. She is a stranger here and on her own. We called the number she had scribbled down: wrong number. We checked with our local phone company, Pacific Bell. They said the prefix was a GTE number and GTE then volunteered the 800 service number.

We had an address and tried to get the phone company to use their reverse directory to find our new missing employee's phone number. The first GTE operator was uncooperative and shut the door by saying, "We don't do anything but give out numbers. We don't—" and we hung up. Our theory is . . . we are the customer. We don't have to put up with scolding, static, poor attitudes, negatives, etc. We just hang up.

We redialed the 800 GTE service number. A very pleasant operator put me through to supervisor Mrs. Robaledo, who was perfect: patient, soft, easy. She went off the line, came back and said, "Sir, that number you gave me was one digit off and the number you need is unlisted so the only thing I can do is call that number and request that they call you."

HEY! What modest Mrs. Robaledo is doing . . . is what every customer service guru is trying to teach-do-and-drive-down as a message to Customer Service people! I asked Mrs. Robaledo to whom I should write a Thank You and she said (ready?) . . .

"Oh, sir, you needn't do that. That's what we're here for." Atta way to go, Mrs. Robaledo!

Some people solve problems. Other people create problems.
And the weird thing is . . . they are often in the same Company.

Comments and Extracts—
From a Respected Source

"The Empowerment of Service Workers: What, Why, How and When" by David E. Bowen and Edward R. Lawler III, *Sloan Management Review*, Spring 1992.

Often, WAYMISHes are caused by insensitive and outmoded systems and glitches in procedures. Others can be traced to employees who aren't adequately selected, trained or empowered. Sometimes, WAYMISHes occur when employees are restricted by job definition.

There are major benefits to empowerment.

1. Quicker response to customer needs, at the time the service is being delivered. No delays. No need to ask a supervisor for approval, no retreat behind, "It's not our policy." Only action to satisfy the customer. (Solve the problem.)

2. Quicker responses to unhappy customers. The inevitable snafus or misunderstandings are immediately addressed. If something doesn't go right the first time, the next best thing is for the person at the scene to fix it right away. (Keep the customer.)

   Overdoing it: Caution needs to be exercised in taking care of an unhappy customer if that causes unreasonable delays for others who resent the over-attention being paid to a troublemaker.

   Breaking the rules using a common-sense solution is fine, but unrestricted rule-breaking—which may be the source of heroic stories—can lead to trouble. It should be tempered by good sense to avoid "customer chaos."

3. When employees feel better about their jobs and themselves they treat customers better, stay with the company longer, have less absenteeism (and are less likely to join a union).

4. If empowerment includes participation and welcomes suggestions to the organization, it frees up employees to feel comfortable in suggesting ideas for improvement. It is not a stretch to say that *empowerment equals improvement*. Better service than the competition adds up to stronger customer loyalty, higher sales and lower costs.

But empowerment comes with costs. Usually, empowered employees earn more. If the firm has spent more time selecting and training, there will usually be more fringe benefits. Starbucks includes its part-time employees in its benefit plan. One result: it has one-third lower turnover rate than comparable restaurants. Most successful companies pay above average and get above average productivity—high hourly labor costs translate into disproportionately higher sales per employee!

Here are some variables to take into account as you empower.

The answers to these questions affect the degree of empowerment. Usually there will be less empowerment in the first alternative, more in the second:

1. Is your basic business strategy low cost and high volume? Or a customized, personalized service?
2. How are you tied to the customer—a single transaction? Or a long-term relationship?
3. Is your technology routine, simple and repetitive? Or non-routine and complex?
4. Is your business environment predictable with few surprises? Or is it mercurial and variable?
5. Are your types of people authoritarian managers and employees with low growth and social needs—or—empowering managers and employees with high growth and social needs, and strong interpersonal skills?

When you're buying subway tokens, you want fast, accurate service. But you don't want the subway clerk to be your buddy. When you're looking for a special anniversary gift and you're not sure what's appropriate, you want a knowledgeable, patient, sensitive salesperson. The WAYMISH exposure in giving out subway tokens is limited to accuracy and a minimum of unpleasantness. We don't expect much. But in the second situation, lots can go wrong. When it goes right, the sales person has both made a sale and created a trusting customer.

QUICKIE

Was caravaning back down from a rural town called *Show Low* in Arizona on a heat-busting August afternoon and, by acclamation of the Hellmann clan, stopped for a cooling ice cream.

It was a weekend. It was hot. The Dairy Queen was swarming with families, kids, dads, lines of people.

Ordered a sundae and forgot to tell the server I despise whipped cream. Mile-high slathers of white foamy whipped cream arrived mounted atop the Dairy Queen cup. "Can't do that," I say.

With no more than three seconds hesitation, the server held up the whipped cream sundae to the assembled crowd like a priest elevating a chalice and shouted, "One great sundae at half price!"

The man knows how to solve problems, generate smiles, make an immediate bargain-priced sale and create positive PR for his company.

A LESSON FROM THE PROs

In a seminar on Customer Service, if you ask the audience "What does the Phone Company do when your call doesn't go through?" you usually get a lot of vacant stares and non-answers. You push harder with, "I'm trying to get you to recall how the Phone Company handles a problem." It's funny, but when you spell it out for them (as we are about to do), then they all start nodding their heads "Oh yes! Oh yes! Sure . . . "

CALLER: Operator, I was cut off.

OPERATOR: Sorry, sir. I'll give you credit for your call. Do you wish to place another call? (Snap! Problem solved. Customer taken care of. New business solicited.)

AFTO (Ask For The Order)

How long did that take? Three and a half seconds . . . times X million calls a day. Did the operator hassle the caller, ask for driver's license, a major credit card?

No.

How come?

What are these telephone people trying to do?

Get you to spend more money with them! . . . now . . . while you are happy with a problem solved and a cordial operator asking if she can help you further. That's what.

How about asking your employees, "What are the Best and Quickest instant rebates, immediate make-good, hassle-free returns **they've** experienced with any outside business. . . ."

Or ask them when was the last time they were surprised by outstanding service in any business?

Might be more impressive for them to share real-life experiences than listen to routine company lectures on Treat the Customer Right.

DOING IT RIGHT FOR 70 YEARS

Founded in the 1930s by Arthur Taubman, Advance Auto Stores, Roanoke, VA, is now a chain of more than 2,500 auto parts stores, and still growing. Although the company has changed in many ways, Nick Taubman has never wavered from his father's basic philosophy:

"Every employee has the ability and the power
to satisfy every customer every time."

Supported by every level of management, ingrained in the company's selection, training, promotion, recognition, and communication policies, this 70 year old expression of customer concern and faith in employees shows how the simplest statement can have a far reaching effect on a company's success.

Hundreds of complimentary letters from customers astounded by the level of unexpected service they get from Advance folks are monthly proof that the WAYMISH virus is hard to find in Advance Auto.

Reality Check

Test your policies against what really goes on.

Have your employees answer these questions:

- Am I allowed to do "almost anything" to do a high quality job and satisfy customers?
- Do I have the authority to correct problems as they occur? (It is impossible to have a policy for every contingency.)
- Am I allowed and encouraged to be creative in my work? (How far is *too* far?)
- Do I have to go through a lot of red tape to change a procedure?
- What channels do I have to go through to effect a change I feel is necessary?

Let employees answer anonymously . . . and you will find out how they really feel about their freedom to "do the job."

Positive answers to these questions will not only characterize the WAYMISH-sensitive firm, but prove that Management understands it can't legislate the one-to-one contact between an employee and the customer.

If you don't like the answers, ask yourself some questions: Are you creating an atmosphere of policies favoring empowerment? Or blocking it?

As role models, management comes out, meets customers, works the floor for short periods, publicizes hero stories of outstanding service and relates how these stories kill a WAYMISH in its early stages.

Sending consistent signals that you trust your people and expect them to perform at high standards takes time to be accepted. It takes time for employees to feel that you mean it, that the psychological environment is dependable, that they know clearly where you are going, what is expected of them and what they can do . . . on their own!

Why isn't all management concerned about its people? In some cases, those employees losing power or status (middle managers and some unions) resist change. When times get tough, many managers feel that only centralized toughness will work. They pull all decision-making back to HQ, eliminate training, drive, rather than lead people, and preach rather than listen. They also turn off everybody and in time lose their good people. And the good ones are the first to go.

Getting Acceptance

QUESTION: How do you convey the idea of Empowerment to your employees when they are concerned about exceeding the limits of their authority—and being reprimanded—or fired?

At Nordstrom the rule is, "Treat your customers as you would a friend." At Carl Sewell's car dealership the decision to charge for an extra service is, "Would you charge a friend for this?" In essence, it's Common Sense. But what are the parameters?

If you don't have a highly formalized system like Sewell (his story later), or a culture like Nordstrom, getting acceptance is best done in small groups. How?

Tell stories. True happenings observed in other businesses. Small extras that made a difference. Positive points. Let your people relate to those incidents. Then encourage them to tell Why they do business with certain stores, hairdressers, car dealers, professionals (doctors, CPAs) —and what happened to make them feel that way.

It's the oldest interactive technique in the world: you tell me yours; I'll tell you mine.

And soon we're on the same channel, nodding, agreeing that it's *the small and personal things that make the difference.*

How to Collect the Stories

Easy. Carry a slim pocket-sized WAYMISH note jotter card to write down the small dumb things that annoy **you as the customer** of other businesses—any businesses. (You jot them down because you forget them very quickly.)

Like what?

Not being welcomed. Not being taken care of promptly. Phones answered rudely. Customers put endlessly on Hold. Being ignored by staff members other than the one assigned to you. Being told repeatedly, "Your sales person (waiter, representative, customer service agent) will be with you in a minute." Delays in getting a bill . . .

Then, with your notes, you go back and do your damnedest to make sure these WAYMISHes are **not** happening to **your customers in your business!**

A strong point to make is that the "magic touches" that could be happening in your business **can cost nothing.**

Here are just a few we jotted down on the Positive side:

The warmth of welcome and the personal service over three days by the doorman (P.J. at the Sheraton Boston); the smile and sincerity of the receptionist (Pasadena Ritz Carlton); the graciousness of a maitre d' (Century Plaza dining room); immediate attention and greeting by name with personal limo pick up at LAX airport (Ted's arrival at Ritz Carlton Marina del Rey); the great sense of humor server Caroline dishes up at Barkley's Restaurant.

And in very little time . . . you and your business can build your own list of "magic touches" by your people whose service and attitude will bring back the customer every time.

And for Management

Now the question is: How can *you as Management* find out the kind of almost invisible "touches" **your** customers have experienced as "Ahas" in your business? It isn't easy.

- One way to find out for sure, is for you—whoever you are and at what ever level—to get out of your office and **Talk To Your Customers personally**. (MBWA—Management By Walking Around) Personally call a few every day.
- The other is to insist that some small quick daily meetings are set up—and happen. ["Quick and Daily" because people forget these little points overnight.]

> What was the smallest or simplest thing you found
> that made a difference to a customer today?
> Tell us a compliment you got from a customer today . . .
> What can you think of that particularly pleased one of
> your customers?

And write down the answers!

Why? Because such small successes are overlooked in formalized training . . . and your higher, more sophisticated management echelons may not believe what infinitesimal touches can make your customers happy. Management are Policy People. Manual Mavens. And most of the Magic Touches are not in the book. They happen. And should be captured.

The Non-Secret

The successes of these Magic Touches come under one heading — **ATTITUDE.**

How can employees or managers handle your customers with exceptional style if they are not having some fun doing their job? Or if they don't enjoy dealing with people? Or are not allowed to work in their own style?

The Natural Look

Loosen up, Management. Let your people be themselves. They each have a personality. Some may be as outgoing and personable as a Dale Carnegie graduate. Others may be that quiet-sincere trustworthy type. No one, repeat NO ONE, has ever come up with ONE PROFILE for "the successful sales person."

Training? Yes. Rules—yes. Strictly by the book—we have our doubts. The Good Ones always do it a little differently.

Winners

Superior sales service people come in all sizes. All shapes, heights and widths. And a variety of educational backgrounds. Degrees. And no degrees. Look back in your recent experience. Who are the two Best sales people you can recall? Someone you bought a house from; a car from; clothes from; insurance from. Or just a "clerk" whose Attitude toward serving and helping you was outstanding; someone who made it pleasant for you to buy?

From

The key word is "from." As a customer, you choose whom you want to buy *from*. It is your choice. The more important question is: How can *your business increase those odds so more customers choose You?*

Lee Iacocca said it well when he addressed thousands of his dealers one year in Atlantic City: "I'm not going to tell you how to sell cars! I'm not going to tell you to brag about Chrysler being the first with 50,000 and 70,000 mile warranties . . . I'll just give you the Four Key Words! Ready?"—and he shouted at the top of his lungs . . .

"MAKE SOMEBODY LIKE YOU!!"

Then he added much more softly, "And if they **like** you—they will buy from you. And if they **don't** like you they will find all kinds of reasons **not** to buy from you." Then he summarized with this basic wisdom: "If people like you, they will buy. If you treat them right, they will bring their friends who will buy, and those people will bring their friends. . . ."

Pretty basic stuff from one of America's greatest salesmen—who incidentally, turned a Losing Company into a First Class competitor with—ATTITUDE.

NEGOTIATION
Getting What You Want And What You Deserve

IF YOU FLY YOU'VE PROBABLY seen the colorful in-flight ads for the Karrass Negotiating seminars. Their catchy headline challenges you: "In life you don't get what you deserve... you get what you negotiate." And one key premise of their seminars is... *Find out what's on the other person's page—then negotiate.*

Remember... everything someone put together, can be negotiated (changed) by someone else.

In a WAYMISH situation, try to put yourself on the same side of the problem as the person you are dealing with. These problems often concern Authority. What is the other person's problem or position? In the case of sales people, they are limited in what changes they can make in what they understand to be "policy." That sets up a "barrier to buying" and signals a WAYMISH. And, obviously, going over anyone's head triggers resentment, makes them look bad, and does nothing to create an advocate for your cause. Then it is best to immediately smile, be cordial and say:

"Let's see if together we can come up with an alternative we can both live with."

Suppose you want gift items delivered to three separate addresses. The sales person says that "under our standard procedure" that will require extra charges and a longer delivery schedule. Neither of you wants to change your position (you don't want to pay the extra charges; she feels she has to follow the rules).

You say: *"The problem isn't you or me—it's the policy. Let's see if together we can convince your manager to be more flexible."*

Call the manager, explain the situation, suggesting you and the clerk are together in trying to conclude this sale—on your terms. By making everyone look good (maybe you'll compromise on the extra charges if the deliveries can be made on time) you've increased the odds of getting what you want.

You Cut. I Choose.

In negotiating WAYMISH situations, see if there are reasonable alternatives. From childhood we are used to trading off: I'll let you ride my bike if I can have a chunk of your candy. Or the wise Solomon technique: If we have to divide the last piece of pie, you cut the pie but I will get to choose which slice I want.

When you run into a problem, instead of demanding the whole piece, ask, "What do I have to do and what do you have to do so we come out with something we can *both* accept?"

"Compromise" is not a good word to use during negotiation. It often describes splitting the difference. *Concession is* more appropriate. That means *each* giving up something but each getting a major share of what's important to them. Never compromise your values. As a buyer, you can always walk away, come another day, or go somewhere else.

But even in the press of time to get what you want NOW— don't collapse and capitulate. Try the "I will... if you will" offer. Say, "Look, I really don't have the time to make a federal case out of this. I'd like this item and I'll buy it right now if you will..." and ask for a slightly bigger piece of the pie, a concession. It can't hurt. You *are* the customer.

The I-T-P Formula

The three parts of any negotiation are INFORMATION—what you each want to know about the other and how clear you are about what you want—TIME—deadlines, constraints, pressure to conclude the deal—and POWER—who has the authority and who controls the situation.

A few examples... you go into a store Tuesday afternoon. The department where you want to make your purchase is empty. Two sales clerks. No other customers but you. What information do you now have? Not much if any business is being done. Perhaps you comment, "Things a little bit slow?" If that's confirmed with, "You can say that again!" or "Well, ha ha, there are three of us now," you can feel pretty confident the sales people are likely to be willing to give you what you want.

This is exactly what happened when Bill went into a jewelry store to buy a necklace for his wife. While leisurely making his choice and talking casually, he learned from the two sales women that he was their first customer of the day.

Although the store was known for fixed prices, Bill decided to "go for it." He asked whether they could reduce the price, maybe absorb the sales tax, wrap the necklace in a special gift box, and possibly throw in a pair of earrings? Yes to everything!... because he used the three steps: Information (observing the situation and casual questioning), using the luxury of Time and the complete lack of Pressure.

How to Get Information

By being smart and offering answers? Or by acting puzzled and dumb and getting the other side to "tell you everything?" (What's on their "page.") One of the best negotiators we ever met was this slow-talking Southerner who acted as though he had just fallen out of a hayloft. He claimed not to know or understand ANYTHING!

His Company had gotten into a WAYMISH situation about the meaning of a contract. We thought the contract was clear. After all, our lawyers had drawn it up. Our Southern friend said he didn't understand a word of it. How could he, this country boy? We proceeded to go over every phrase, impatience growing, as he questioned the meaning, motivation, intent, ramifications, choice of words, even some punctuation!

When we got through with a complete explanation, HE knew every part of our strategy. WE knew nothing of his! Moral: Ask ask ask. Then listen and act as dumb as you can.

Time's on Your Side

Time can often work in your favor. Suppose you have a misunderstanding with a sales person or cashier and there is a considerable line of customers waiting to be served. You have a problem—replacing a shop-worn item, checking to be sure you have the latest model, whatever. You act as though you have all the time in the world, as if this is your only chore of the day.

Obviously, time is on your side. The sales person is under pressure from other impatient customers, or a manager is observing the transactions, or her commission income could be slipping away if other customers aren't served. It will help you get what you want if you are not arrogant and don't completely monopolize her time.

The Time Trap

Deadlines are indeed deadly to good negotiations. They almost always work against the party who is under the gun for time. So try to recognize and walk away from situations where you see the decided advantage is on the other side. Go away and come back when you have the freedom of time to negotiate on your terms.

And don't give away your deadlines! "Oh gosh—I have to pick up the kids at 3 o'clock sharp; I'm late, so we have to settle this in five minutes." Uh uh. Not the start of a smart negotiation strategy. Whatever the issue, you're likely to settle for less than you would with time in your favor (or make it appear to be). And you are letting yourself in for that maddening regret later: Why did I make the foolish mistake of rushing into this with so little time?

You Have the Power

Power is yours *when you use it*. As a buyer, the ultimate weapon is to walk away. IF you can live without the purchase/service/accommodation, always put that power of NOT buying into your consideration.

There is a big difference between a *want* and a *need*. (Needs are eating, sleeping, and drinking). You *want* a shirt, tie, or sports jacket but you don't *need* any of them today. And that goes for automobiles, too (there are always rentals if your car has died).

You want the WAYMISH situations solved without strong-arm, secret police tactics. Threats may work but they rarely leave the right taste in anyone's mouth and outright threats almost always ruin the possibility of continuing relationships.

Most of us want smooth, easy, agreeable interactions in a buying-selling situation. So when power is an element in settling a WAYMISH use it gently. "I'd like to buy this suit but we seem to be apart on the cost of the alterations, delivery, and something you could throw in, like a tie. After all, it is quite a lot of money—$475. I know I could go across the street to your competitor where I've already looked, but I like the way you've handled this. How do you suggest we resolve it so I can buy from you?"

Then be quiet. Shut up and look at the sales person. You've served the ball into the other court. You've made it clear you have options, and you've also shown you favor this store if they're willing to discuss alternatives. Pause. Give the seller a chance to be creative and to save face (important in any culture). Power in this case is neither intimidation nor cheating. It's getting what you want—and making a sale for them.

Can You Do It?

All of us know someone in our personal association who's good at negotiating. Sure you do. You know they've gotten terrific bargains under the sticker price by paying cash on a refrigerator at Sears, saved $85 on a piece of jewelry in a high-fashion store by making the manager an offer, had auto dealers add on a couple of hundred dollars worth of extras and driven out with a marvelous deal. It amazed you. Where do they get the nerve?

Sure, if you're not used to negotiation it's a little scary, but think of it this way:

You know what you want, it's in your mind.
Getting it *out of your mind* and into negotiating is simply ASKING!

About Power

In democratic America, power is rarely discussed openly. Presidential candidates never campaign to be elected so they can wallow in the power and privileges of the position.

With parents, only when they feel they're losing the argument with their kids do they resort to, "You'll do it because I'm your father and I said so!"

As a customer, no one can tell you what you have to do. You can always negotiate, or walk. So the WAYMISH works both ways. Businesses put up what we call "barriers to buying" rules, regulations, stipulations etc., that make it difficult for us to give them our money. This creates the customer's challenge: getting yourself out of WAYMISH situations. Here are some aspects of power that will help you negotiate.

COMPETITION—Everybody has some competitor. The more you know about this company's competitor the more careful the seller will be not to exaggerate claims, and be more interested in finding out how much *you* know about the product. It's OK to use the competitors as leverage. Let it be known you can shop elsewhere. Or you can do nothing. The more options you have, the stronger your negotiating position.

LEGITIMACY—"That's what it said in your ad"; "That's what the lady on the phone said when I called"; "I talked to someone named Jenkins and he said—": "Funny, every other company in your business includes that at no charge." These phrases are references to an authoritative voice that help your position when you feel the rules need to be stretched or changed.

EXPERTISE—Whenever you are in a position to apply your special skill or knowledge, that's a negotiating edge. Talking with authority using technical phrases not known to the general public helps. Asking questions that probe will show that you know the industry or product and will gain the respect of the seller in terms of treating you fairly.

TRADE OFFS—If the seller knows you have a need (machinery replacement, a lease ending, an inventory deadline approaching, emergency shipments), he feels *he* has the power. Like the fabled heroes in the movies—stay cool. Think "out-of-the box." Get creative. Don't give up unless you get something back! Remember the "I-will-if-you-will" motto.

IDENTIFICATION—the more the seller sees you as a reliable, moral, decent person, the greater your chances that you will be treated with respect and fairness. Your demeanor, poise, conversation, language and willingness to listen all project the image that you may well be an important customer to this business. Impression generates negotiation points for you.

Finally, PERSISTENCE—in asking many successful people (managers, CEOs, negotiators, superior sales people) what characterizes successful negotiators, we found everyone included persistence, not giving up, staying on target, hanging in there. It wouldn't be surprising if a research study showed that stubbornness is more effective than brilliance in getting what you want.

What Does NO Mean?

People get upset when they hear "No." It shuts their minds down. It equals defeat. Maybe this reaction has to do with our early training, parental and school discipline. But consider expanding your understanding of the word. It may just mean, "I don't understand."

Or No may mean, "What you're saying doesn't sound very attractive. Add something exciting to this offer." Or, "No, but let me ask you some questions..." may be a first reaction leading to a more thorough consideration and questioning. In negotiating, don't immediately take No as a definite anti-position. It is often just a stopping place along the road to further negotiation through persuasion.

Issuing an Ultimatum

Herb Cohen (marvelous speaker, international negotiator and author of *You Can Negotiate Anything)* suggests four criteria before using an ultimatum:

1. *Only at the end of the negotiation.* When there is no other choice. Or when the investment of the other side has been so great it is now impossible for them to walk away.

2. *Face-saving.* Never belittle or offend. Doing so may infuriate the other side and lose any advantage you've gained. State your position and reasons. Ask them how they can help bring this impasse to a conclusion.

3. *Support your position with legitimacy.* Like the lawyer, use documents, tradition, equity, industry standards, lore, the Bible, a contract, a not-to-exceed budget, accounting and financial records.

4. *Either/Or.* The final alternative. Tell the other side, "You choose This or That, either is acceptable to me." It stops the arguing. Puts the decision totally in their hands. Famed child psychologist Haim Ginott preached what works with kids, works with adults: "Do you want orange or grapefruit juice? Eggs scrambled or hard boiled? Do you want to go to bed at 8:00, or 8:15?" Giving away the choice when either option is acceptable—is very powerful negotiation.

Can We Fly United?

Okay, here's a case where Information, Time and Power were not available but the result was positive because the WAYMISH became "personal."

Harry and Mary were booked on a business-class flight from New York to Rome. Their taxi to JFK airport was delayed in traffic. They arrived at 6:45 for what their tickets said was an 8:00 PM flight. Plenty of time. NO! The departure time had been changed to 7:15.

They had not been called, and had seen no reason to check the flight schedule. Their seats had been given away (according to strict airline policy), and there were only two separate seats available in coach.

Mary told the gate agent this trip was the first part of their honeymoon, a second marriage between two sixty-year-olds and she would be heartbroken if she couldn't sit next to Harry. Minutes later the agent quietly conducted the honeymooners to adjoining first class seats. Hooray! And then the surprise: the attendants poured champagne for all first class passengers and led a welcome song, "Happy Wedding to You."

What Are the Lessons?

Don't collapse at the first sign of disappointment or refusal. Don't argue, shout and point fingers. (Why didn't the airline or travel agent call? Who dares give away our seats? What do you mean we have to fly in coach? We paid for business class!) First, get on the plane. Be calm (Remember the power of Identification—decent, well-behaved, mature people.) Make the problem a personal one, not an airline problem.

Shouting, threatening, complaining publicly is a sure way to raise the hackles and the resolve of the employee gatekeepers (the ones who have the power to turn the key and let you in). And bullying behavior challenges them to put you in your place and refuse to change the rules.

Besides... who could turn down a tearful new bride of sixty some?

Play It Again

Chet wanted to buy an electronic keyboard to take with him on a trip to Florida where he was going to visit his ailing eighty-year-old brother-in-law. It was New Year's Eve. Early in the afternoon, Chet visited a music store, investigated several instruments and, after checking with a clerk that the store would be open until 5:00 PM, left with some descriptive material.

At 4:15 he returned, ready to buy the keyboard. The door was locked, the sign turned to read CLOSED. Inside employees were getting ready to leave for the holiday. Chet banged on the door. Someone inside waved that international signal: store closed. Chet banged again, mouthing that he wanted to speak to the manager, who opened the door a crack and re-announced they were closed for New Year's.

Chet told the manager he'd returned because a salesman had promised (interesting word in negotiating) that the store would be open until 5:00. More important, Chet said, he needed the keyboard to brighten his depressed brother-in-law who might be inveigled into singing with the keyboard (Add a little emotion).

"I know the model I want and I have a credit card (holding it up in the face of the manager as his documentation)... and you can make a quick extra $260 sale." Ha! That did it. The manager let Chet in, wrapped the keyboard, swiped the credit card and rang up the final sale of the business year.

Lesson (again): Personalize the problem. Use the nine Magic Words: *I have a problem and I need your help.* Describe a credible need. Act decently. Make it easy for the seller.

Who won? Everybody.

Investment

Time can often work in your favor because it creates an economic and emotional involvement on the part of both parties. The longer you and any salesperson discuss a deal, examine alternatives, debate values, the harder it is for either of you to just let it drop.

For example, we urge clients who are thinking of selling their businesses to identify possible buyers months, even years before they're ready to put the company on the block. Invite potential buyers in for a look, have them sign confidentiality agreements, send them financial statements every quarter, ask them for advice. Then when you get down to brass tacks—negotiating the actual sale—it will definitely be difficult for any serious buyer to extract himself from the bidding process.

Similarly, the longer you involve any salesperson in the purchase process—questions about details, coming back more than once, calling for additional information—the easier it will be for you to resolve any

WAYMISH when you get down to the actual buying step. You both will be thinking, "Hey—look how much time I have in this already..." That's a plus for you, Mr. or Ms. WAYMISH-warrior.

Use the Echo Technique

Repeat the points the other party has made. It shows respect and you're more likely to answer intelligently. Repeating the other person's words aloud may cause him to "hear" that his proposition or refusals are extreme or impractical and could be modified.

"Even though the envelope was postmarked eight days before my credit card payment was due, and only across town—because the post office messed up and delivered it here two days late—are you *really* going to charge me interest?" Restating the complete scenario highlights the unreasonableness of it and helps clear the way for a fair solution.

Ah, the Bully

If you feel you're being bullied and realize there is little chance of coming to an agreement—walk off with a smile and wave good-bye. Interesting reactions come from the bullies: they hate to face the failure of their tactics. Often, they will say, "Hey! Where are you going? We're not finished here—" You have now begun to recapture your leverage and can decide whether to continue or attack from a different angle: by going to a higher level and reporting your experience to management.

And take names. If you saw the movie "Schindler's List," you'll remember Liam Neeson's technique of dealing with the Nazi bullies: out with a notepad and pen, "Your name is . . . T." Standing up to these antagonists threatens them with exposure to higher authority and immediately levels the playing field.

Keep a Sharp Eye

Watch for the clues which indicate meanings different from the expressed words. The inadvertent slip—inappropriate word, change of tone, falter in voice—that tells you there is more behind the words being said. When someone has been looking you in the eyes for the past ten minutes, then drops his eyes, turns aside, fumbles with a pen, spills some coffee, screws up his shoulders, clears his throat or tightens his voice, you don't have to be a clinical psychologist to realize you're not getting the whole story.

There are several styles of negotiating. And yes, a bully can win by being a yeller, a screamer, KGB inquisitor, or dominating the discussion by talking LOUDER than anyone else. But watching the reactions of others temporarily cowered by this blast of power, you see people waiting to get their revenge.

"Don't burn your bridges" is old and good advice. Most of us prefer solutions that are fair, benefit both parties, and leave a good feeling and the possibility of positive relationships. That's why we say in WAYMISH: *Make it easier to do business.* Because that's what people want.

Battling the Bureaucracy

In our dealings, sooner or later we all face the "giants"—banks, utilities, hospitals, the city, cable companies, etc. First rule: *get the name* of the person you are speaking with ("Schindler's List" again). Get out a piece of paper and a pen. Ask specifically for the spelling of the name (this adds a note of serious intent). Get a title, department, to whom they report. (This will signal that you are not just some ordinary complaining customer.) Often you will get a whole new hearing when the other person recognizes the importance for *them* of settling this issue now.

If no solution emerges, follow up with a concise letter. If there is a claim number, a case file or report number, print and underline those numbers. That is a further sign you mean business. Next, *clearly* state your problem at the very beginning of your letter, and take the time to review your words. Make the description crisp and to the point. No rambling. No editorials. Like the old "Dragnet" TV series, give "the facts, ma'am, just the facts."

Point: Your letter has to "sell" some unknown clerk to help you. Think of the beleaguered clerk handling a mishmash of garbled long-winded complaints. Make it EASY for that clerk to do her job. Tempt her to pick out your letter as an easy one to solve. Isn't it human nature to start with the easy ones?

Checking Up

Be sure your note asks for a decision by a specific *date*. That will put you in a Time category in their system. Next, call before that date asking how the problem-solving is progressing. This is an unsubtle way of not letting them off the hook. While you're at it, use the name of the person you started with, or enlist a new advocate for your cause. Remember, these are the people who are yelled at, cursed, abused. A touch of friendly persuasion goes a long way toward getting the gate-keeper to relinquish impersonal treatment, and act in a friendly manner.

Working Together

A collaborative solution to a WAYMISH requires a building of trust. And that begins at the pre-opening stages of the negotiations— gaining commitment (based on the other party's position) and the cordial handling of early objections. As in most human relationships, you get what you give. But in a WAYMISH situation, if the issue is important to you, it is unlikely to be as important to the other person. So stick with it. You *are* the customer.

IT'S OUR POLICY

Is that Good? Or Bad? Depends . . .

THE COMPANY RULES

T ED VISITED A 1,200-employee plant and saw twenty-six rules plastered all over the walls. He asked the CEO why, when God gave Moses only ten rules, this CEO needed twenty-six. In a few minutes, they reduced the number of rules to four—

- No drugs or alcohol
- No lying
- No stealing
- Only first-rate quality

QUESTION THE RULES

A WAYMISH can come from a perversion of what seemed originally like a good idea. The old saw that "no good deed goes unpunished" is probably the source of many WAYMISH problems. Here's one by Norm Brodsky from the June 1997 *INC*. magazine:

The uncle of Norm's wife had done business with a car dealer for many years. When he went to pick up his car after it had been repaired and asked to test-drive it to see that the repair had been done properly before paying for it, he was told by a service employee that he couldn't take the car out of the place until the bill had been paid. Catch 22? The company rule had been established because someone (probably long ago) had stuck the dealer with an unpaid repair bill.

To Norm's uncle the rule was a sign of distrust. He called the owner who apologized and took care of the problem—AFTER making a good customer unhappy, an employee look bad, and causing himself annoyance and embarrassment.

What's the lesson? Think through the implications of all rules. Are they set up to take care of general problems or conditions, or to handle the rare, but disturbing situation? Do they restrain or punish the few targeted transgressors or do they attack the majority of customers and employees who are unlikely ever to violate or even test the rules? Do you set up rules to avoid having employees apply judgment because you don't trust them or haven't trained them?

Tough questions, but worth asking and answering in your anti-WAYMISH campaign.

THE WIZ AND THE WAYMISH

Customer bought a 27-inch TV set at The Wiz, a chain of appliance, electronic stores in New York City. Total bill came to about $700, including tax and delivery. Customer asks for delivery the next Friday and asks The Wiz salesman what time the delivery would be made.

The Wiz says, "Some time between 9 A.M. and 6 P.M." Customer laughs and says, "How about a slightly more precise two- to three-hour window of time?"

Wiz salesman responds, "If you want to know a more specific time you should call the delivery-service number on Thursday night or early Friday morning."

Customer gets serious and suggests, "For $700 please ask them to call me."

"Our policy is not to call."

"For $700, how about changing your policy when I ask you to make it easier for us to get delivery?"

He said he would look into it—but couldn't promise.

Don't sound like no Wiz to us . . . Don't you want my money? Doesn't your management want the money?

Do you really believe the people on top, the ones who put together this chain of stores, would have a policy like that: We don't call?

(WIZ filed for bankrupty in late 1997!)

For Management—some questions:

(a) Are any of your employees making their own rules for Customer Service?

(b) Who in your organization is supposed to be tuned to what is happening—actually happening— at the levels of contact with your customers?

(c) Is any one of your management walking around, talking around the check-outs, delivery, shipping or complaint points?

(d) Are you?

(e) When was the last time you talked to customers, visited, or best of all, "worked the floor" of your business for a couple of hours?

[Not nasty. Just questions . . .]

HOOK IT UP HAROLD, WE GOT A LIVE ONE!

Went out on a Saturday to L.A. Tronics in Huntington Beach (Calif.) to buy audio speakers for my patio. Walked into the store where a sales(?) person was leaning on the counter talking to a fellow employee standing behind the counter. No acknowledgment of me as a possible buyer, so I walked through the store to the speaker showroom.

There was a customer dickering with a sales(?) clerk about the price of a damaged "as-is" advertised speaker. After about one minute with the horse-trading customer, the clerk looked at me and said, "I'll be right back." I never saw him again.

After shopping for fifteen minutes, I wandered out to find a clerk, a salesperson, a somebody! Eventually, I spotted a clerk behind a counter showing portable speakers to another customer. I walked up to the counter some two feet away from the transaction and waited my turn. [No acknowledgment whatsoever.]

When the clerk was finished with the transaction, he walked past me as though I wasn't there. I am six feet three and weigh about 200 pounds. At the other end of the counter/showcase two clerks were playing with an electronic video game. I walked out of the store.

After checking with my wife to make sure that I had not suddenly turned transparent, I went across town to a Good Guys store and spent $1,000 on speakers.

Being stubborn (and a sales trainer), the next week I went back to the L.A. Tronics store and was introduced to the Area Manager. I walked him through the store pointing out the specific sales(?) people and the places I had visited. I told him of spending $1,000 at the Good Guys store. He nodded his head wisely to one side, smiled and told me in a confidential tone, "We don't like to have our people bother a customer. When they find what they want, we'll answer their questions and sell them the merchandise."

Whoa! A whole new radical approach to Sales: Let the customer sell himself! I couldn't believe it—was this area guy making this up?

Still determined to tell Somebody, I called the main office in San Fernando Valley, and was cycled through their automated electronic answering maze over and over again without ever reaching a human being. (Are you listening management?) I tried on subsequent days, got the same voice mail run-around. I quit! I surrender. All of these sales (?) companies deserve whatever happens to them.*

HELLO???

Ordered a phone from Southern New England Telephone (Connecticut phone company). They sent the wrong color. When purchaser called, they told her to bring it to their Danbury store to exchange. When she asked for the phone number—to find out their hours—she was informed that they didn't accept phone calls! So the phone company refused to give me the phone number for their own store.

Reminds us of the old joke about the phone company:

---

*Since this book was first published, L.A. Tronics closed its door. My, my.

CUSTOMER: "Hello. I'd like to get an unlisted number."

OPERATOR: "No problem, sir. The number will be 456 7890."

CUSTOMER: "Let me ask 2 questions—Will it be published? (no); and can I use the number today? (yes).

CUSTOMER: "Operator—I forgot to write the number down when you gave it to me. Would you repeat it please?"

OPERATOR: "Sorry sir, that number is unlisted."

Same mentality. But no joke in business.

The second episode deals with Paragon, the sporting goods store on 18th Street and Broadway, New York City. When a customer called to order two tennis rackets and gave his VISA number he was told it was "against the law" to take orders over the phone. WOW.

We'll have to check with telephone pal Rudy Oetting and ask him how many BILLIONS were logged on 800 lines last year. We got a *bunch* of companies breaking the law here!

VERGING ON THE RIDICULOUS

A new resident in Oakland, California was concerned about a lost postal package. She consulted the local phone book and under "Government—Post Office," she found a number for U.S. POST OFFICE—Lost & Found. She calls the listed number.

A voice answers. "Post Office . . . "

"Lost and found?" asks the new resident.

"No, we don't have a Lost and Found," says a calm, bureaucratic voice.

Momentarily stunned, the caller hesitates, recovers and says unbelievingly, "You don't *have* a Lost and Found? Then how come it's listed in the phone book?"

"So we can tell people we don't have one," says the voice and hangs up.

TURN AROUND

The Man took over a failing airline. He studied the competition. He was appalled at the attitude—lack of attitude—all the airlines, including his own, had toward the customers. Treating them cavalierly was the norm. Surveying the possible markets, he saw the business people flying back and forth from Scandinavia to the Continent as a hugely profitable market if—IF he could attract them with focused personal service, flights that suited their business schedules.

He did two things:

One, by reviewing every step of the customer-contact procedure, he saw five critical times when the customer would be satisfied—or he would lose that customer to another airline.

He called these five points of contact "the Moments of Truth." Details in a minute.

Two, he asked his customers: *What Time Would You Like to Get There?* and then adjusted his flights to meet their best arrival schedules to and from the Continent.

This do-what-the-customer-wants move won him a huge chunk of that higher-profit bizniz-traveler market from his more rigidly structured competitors.

Details

A "Moment of Truth" identifies the five basic contact points where airline and customer meet: making a reservation; getting tickets; boarding; flying; and retrieving baggage.

At any one of these "Moments of Truth," CEO Jan Carlzon lectured over and over, is where "We can keep, strengthen or lose a customer!" And he was an evangelist on how with one, one insensitive dumb move you can lose even a loyal customer, FAST.

And as part of this strategy, he empowered his people to "make good" on the spot—no forms to fill out, no higher permission to be sought. Just Do It. (He trusted the judgment of mature people.)

With equal fervor, Carlzon preached that *missing* the opportunity to serve the customer as perfectly as possible at every "Moment of Truth" meant giving the customer a choice of three or four other competing airlines.

From this, consider these two questions in your business:

QUESTION #1: **Are you asking your customers how they would like you to operate** . . . *so they can give you more of their money?*

QUESTION #2: **What are the Moments of Truth in your business?**

It would be worth identifying them, publishing them—and checking up on them constantly.

[If an SAS plane was late arriving in Paris from Stockholm, the pilot's first chore was to answer the airport phone and explain to the Chairman, Mr. Carlzon, why the plane was late!]

MAKING WHOOPEE . . . AND MONEY

If most of what you offer is a commodity, differentiate your company's product and service by making every customer contact more pleasant, helpful, and fun. Make it easier to do business with you.

Southwest Airlines has put the fun back in flying. A *lot* more fun than United or American! They have the same equipment, schedules, and better food (because they don't serve any!). On one flight, they hid a very small female attendant in the overhead bin. She popped out and yelled, "Hey! Glad to have you on board!"

Southwest doesn't serve food or champagne but the flight crew will put together a paper bag full of nuts and maybe a few mini-bottles of vodka and have the attendants sign the bag, then announce a birthday on the P.A. system and have the entire plane sing, "Happy Birthday Dear E-Liz-a-Beth —Happy Birthday to you!"

Think they're crazy? OK. Go stand in the *long* lines waiting to board unassigned seats. Or take a look at their ticketless ticket system. Your reservation code—YTWX7FG9. That's it. You can scrawl it on the back of a scrap of paper, show it to the Southwest counterperson, who will give you a plastic boarding pass (which they take back as you board) and you're in the air. No complex ticket forms. No stacks of perforated paper with a zillion numbers on it in triplicate. Nothing. Have your number—fly. Want a receipt? Just ask any counterperson along the way and get a single slip of paper with the flight, date and price.

As somebody said, "We're back to where we started. Get a reservation. Grab a seat. Go." And Southwest seems to keep on going . . . going . . . going.

On Queue

Unoccupied time feels longer than occupied time
Pre-process waits feel longer than in-process waits
Anxiety makes waits seem longer
Uncertain waits are longer than known, finite waits
Unexplained waits are longer than explained waits
Unfair waits are longer than equitable waits
The more valuable the service, the longer people wait
Solo waiting feels longer than group waiting*

(COURTESY DAVID MEISTER)

Try to remember your own waiting experience and you'll confirm Meister's principles. Some post offices have signs that tell you how many minutes before you reach a postal clerk. Metro North at Grand Central Station in New York has experimented with a clock that tells you how many minutes you'll wait before you reach a ticket window.

Amusement parks make waiting a Game. They find that customers are less ornery when they're kept moving—even if it's from one snake-like line to another. At banks, people prefer one line feeding into multiple tellers to the risk of getting behind a customer with a long transaction.

---

*You might want to copy this list and distribute it to the people in your company who wait on the people who do business with you.

Because people often revere their physicians, they don't gripe as much about sitting in a waiting room as they do about standing in line at the supermarket checkout. Everybody resents a line crasher because it's "Unfair!"

Studies have shown that (1) if actual waiting time is four minutes, people think they've waited for five, (2) a five-minute wait is acceptable, (3) distractions like a TV screen or even a clock make waiting time less boring and customers less likely to gripe.

Here are some suggestions:

- Find out how long is too long—five minutes may be okay in a supermarket, but is totally unacceptable on the phone. Once you know what an acceptable time is, you can measure and monitor it and work on more acceptable solutions.
- Distract and entertain: light, piped-in music, live musicians, entertaining TV monitors. People who are listening and watching are less fidgety and more relaxed.
- Get customers out of line. In New York City and Los Angeles, you can reserve your movie tickets by phone in advance and pick up tickets without waiting in the normal ticket-buying line. ATM machines are impersonal, but they rarely require the waiting time a normal banking queue does.
- Use clocks to inform people of their expected waiting times ONLY when their perceptions are off target. The Meister study showed that people were aware of how long they wait in a bank line. Five minutes was found to be OK. But your service has to meet your promise. If a clock makes customers aware that it's more time than that, the plan backfires!
- Informing customers of off-peak hours reduces queuing. Airlines have spread traffic this way for ages. Other service organizations could offer incentives for doing business off-peak.
- Keep people who aren't serving customers out of sight. When the post office or bank has ten windows and customers see ten clerks with only seven windows open, customers are not happy!
- All customers don't need the same service. Hotels have developed special programs to encourage and reward frequent guests and to get them through registration and check-out procedures faster.

- It takes a long time to change customers' perceptions of service. One-shot approaches are a waste and will soon be forgotten.
- An empathetic, friendly employee can overcome lots of system problems. Hire people who like people and while you continue to upgrade your systems, never stop training and rewarding the behavior you want.

What's The Policy For You?

Outstanding companies develop procedures which first ensure the process works and then teach employees how to operate the process in a foolproof way.

It took years before management analysts figured out that McDonald's success was not only based on providing cheap food in clean, friendly surroundings but, more subtly, on operating systems which institutionalized service and quality **under precise measurable standards.**

How else can you account for consistent service all over the world with a largely temporary workforce?

Another Approach

Taco Bell has tried a different approach in the same marketplace: reduce the number of management levels; develop teams to run individual restaurants, often without a unit manager. Then give these teams the authority to track and order inventory, hire and train new members, handle customer requests, and decide on action to improve things based on their own analysis of their store's P & L.

Which approach is best for you? The answer is a matter of philosophy and trust. How important do you consider consistency?

One Time—or Long Time?

Is your customer contact primarily an individual one-time transaction, or the beginning of a relationship?

If your business is largely one-time customers, then rigorous, consistent standard treatment may be best—and all the customer expects.

But if longer relationships are critical, you may have to empower employees to handle the uniqueness of the transaction—and spend time to develop relationships.

Whichever system you choose, get it right. If the system **works**, employees will be successful from the start and motivated to do the right thing every time.

Dick Lochridge points to Honda and its relationship-building: the salesman doesn't get his commission until the customer signs the delivery check-list.

Finally . . . Process improvement comes *before* training and customer satisfaction.

First, decide on the type and level of service you want to deliver to your customers. Then, determine the best way to deliver it consistently. Lastly, train your people in the process and monitor how your customers feel about what you are doing.

AND THERE ARE WAYS TO DO IT RIGHT

(All you have to do . . . is count 1-2-3)

AN EXPERIENCED consultant begins working with a multiple-stores retailer. Among the array of retail outlets are several Hallmark card shops.

The consultant, like all good consultants, immediately begins to investigate this business: what level of sophistication the employees have; how they interact with a major marketer like Hallmark; how do you motivate and train minimum-wage people?

And the consultant discovers:

A. Hallmark is a remarkable marketing-strategy company.
B. Hallmark assumes nothing.
C. Their year-long printed week-by-week planning calendars are simplified genius.
D. They print out exactly the words they want the retail clerks to say to the customers. *By the day. By the week.*

SUMMARY: This system can apply to **any business**—like yours.
You, too, can teach the rhythm of *1-2-3 step selling.*

Step 1—Acknowledge all customers within 10 seconds of coming into the sightline of the employee or on the phone.

Greeting can be a wave of the hand, a nod, a smile, a tilt of the head, "Hello," "Hi," "Be right with you . . . " Any phrase that's comfortable for the personal style of the retail clerk. Very important phrase: **comfortable for the personal style of the employee.**

When you are training people (especially at near-minimum wage), make it easy for them. Natural. Non-threatening. You're *not* changing them. You're *coaching* them.

Getting basic employees to come out of their shell (except for those rare enthusiastic "natural sales reps") and begin to greet customers is NOT a one-time training class.

And it won't happen by showing a video tape or handing out an instruction sheet.

It takes *constant* managerial Coaching/Reminding/Encouragement on the sales floor, personally and individually urging staff to "Use Step One." But the payoff is terrific.

Think like a shopper for a moment. You know what a feeling you get when you are immediately acknowledged—not by one, but several employees. As you pass by their stations and they acknowledge you, you think, I'm WELCOME here! These people want my business!

Step 2—The Selling Sentences: "What's New"

And here Hallmark publishes a short phrase that becomes the **Selling Sentence** for *that* week. The sentence is printed and distributed. Everybody uses it. You can't avoid it. May be phrased in slightly different words by different employees—but you sure get the message wherever you stop in that store about "what's hot" this week!

Next week, the Selling Sentence changes. New sentence. Fresh angle, different words to promote this week's special Hallmark collectable, coffee mugs, whatever. Great idea!

This keeps employees charged up with new, brief, easy-to-remember one sentence scripts. And that generates extra enthusiasm in their selling. They KNOW what to say. No fumbling or mumbling trying to find the right words. This sentence approach builds employee confidence. Makes them feel at ease. And how can a zeroed-in, concentrated barrage of pre-prepared selling sentences NOT increase sales? It will.

Step 3—Capturing the Customer

With our Greetings and our Selling Sentences we've caught the

Customer's attention. Now we want to make sure she/he doesn't get away, can't escape, without buying.

The key is to train your people to . . . *Be alert.*

Show them how to keep *scanning* their area, sweeping their eyes quickly back and forth. (The same way you scan for shoplifters.)

When you see a customer you "just saw" a few minutes ago, who is now passing your counter, immediately ask: **"Did you find what you were looking for?"**

If they didn't, get out from behind the counter and help them find it! Take them to another section. Don't just point. Those customers wander off *toward* the area you pointed to, are too often confused, not knowledgeable about how you stock items. Take them TO the item. Pick it up and sell it to them!

This happens in banking, too. Hours of surveillance showed customers interested in a loan (big profits for the bank) who were *pointed* to the Loan Department started in that direction, hesitated, turned and *walked out!*

Walked out—profit gone. Customer gone. Is it too much trouble to take a customer to the person who can book the order? (The Ritz Carlton Hotel *escorts* guests to their destination.)

If the other section is too far for you to stray, relay the customer to a fellow employee who can take over—and make that sale.

Now . . . think of yourself again as a shopping customer. How many times in your shopping life has someone in a store "recognized" you after you'd been in the store, asked if you found what you wanted, or offered to get it for you?

That would be what Stew Leonard calls a "WOW!" experience.

It's impressive to be hailed as you are walking out as well as in. It creates such a strong "we-want-your-business" feeling. Capturing the customer *works.*

Try it—you'll like it!

The 1-2-3 system can be applied to any retail operation, and can be modified for any selling situation. Hey! Get up! Ride shotgun on the money express!

It works.

Don't You Want to Know???

Never in the 100 plus supermarkets we've shopped all over the country has one of these markets offered a survey of Customer Satisfaction at check-out. [If you have one, we admire you.]

Nor did the stores we were in solicit comments on the Pluses or Minuses of shopping in their store. WHY NOT?

Are supermarkets different from Hyatt Hotels, United Airlines, Nordstrom, Bloomingdale's or L.L. Bean? Those industry leaders are noted for pro-actively showing their concern about how their customers perceive them and their service.

In this day of fierce competition and cutthroat merchandising, you should **encourage** complaints . . . **ask** for trouble . . . **find out** where the WAYMISHes are . . . **prevent** unhappy customers from walking out your automatic doors and never coming back.

SOLUTION: Have a simple customer survey folder with a return postage permit at your check-out stands, or in your order acknowledgments or invoices, so the customers can tell YOU how THEY feel about your service . . . and WHY they are happy or unhappy.
[Pay to get it back; it'll pay you back!]

Guidelines

A few approaches to asking customers what they want and how you're doing—regardless of the source of the information (interviews, written or phone surveys, focus groups):

1. **Track overall satisfaction with your company.** But remember, feedback on overall satisfaction or dissatisfaction is not actionable. Just a guidepost.
2. **Determine and then track each quality requirement.** You have to know specifically what customers want and—if you can

get to them—what non-customers want. (Survey sample in the back of the book).

3. **Don't neglect broad trends.** Not just your business statistics and patterns, but data about how people are changing *their* buying patterns in general.

4. **Consider how you are going to change** to make it easier, not harder for them to buy from you.

GO WHERE THE CUSTOMERS ARE

A CEO of a national jewelry chain studying trends noticed that shopping malls had peaked as a percentage of total retail sales. Surveys revealed that people were sometimes uncomfortable and felt unsafe in the huge parking lots, didn't like walking long distances within the mall for the one store they wanted to shop in.

Being an alert marketer, the CEO tested locating their stores in smaller strip malls and in stand-alone locations. With lower rents, the new stores were three times as spacious as the mall stores, more convenient for customers, with more inventory and more salespeople.

The success of these changes and trend-aware location decisions not only grew the jewelry chain rapidly, but attracted a renowned investor who paid millions to buy out this trend-aware merchandiser. (Helzberg Jewelry now belongs to Warren Buffett, an avid trend watcher himself.)

ANCIENT CHINESE SECRET

In China, the treatment of customers is so poor the Government has instituted a nationwide Politeness Campaign. Its purpose: to ban the phrases deemed insulting to the customers of retail shops, hotels and airports.

It would be heartless to deprive our readers of this wisdom. So here are 30 of the now government-banned customer-service phrases.

1. What does this have to do with you?
2. If you don't like it, go somewhere else.
3. Ask somebody else.
4. Didn't you hear me? What do you have ears for?
5. That's just the way things are!
6. I don't care who you complain to.
7. Are you finished talking?
8. If you're not buying, what are you looking at?
9. Buy it if you can afford it, otherwise get out of here.
10. Are you buying or not? Make up your mind!
11. What are you yelling about?
12. Don't you see I'm busy? What's your hurry?
13. Hurry up and pay.
14. I just told you. Why are you asking again?
15. Don't stand in the way.
16. Why didn't you choose well when you bought it?
17. Go ask the person who sold it to you.
18. If you don't like it, talk to the manager.
19. Time is up. Be quick.
20. The price is posted. Can't you see it yourself?
21. No exchanges. That's the rule.
22. If you're not buying, don't ask.
23. We haven't opened yet. Wait a while.
24. I'm not in charge. Don't ask me so many questions.
25. I have no change. Go get some yourself.
26. If you want it, speak up; if you don't, get out of the way. Next!
27. Don't talk so much. Say it quickly.
28. Why don't you have the money ready?
29. Get at the end of the line!
30. Stop shouting. Can't you see I'm eating?

Questions about the enforcement of violations of this list should be directed to your local Chinese embassy.

TAKE MY MONEY —PLEASE!

It ain't always easy

BOOK 'EM DANO!

Hauser Chocolates—one of the best mail-order chocolate houses in the country, is where this customer has spent hundreds of happy dollars for dark truffles.

Customer calls, tells the lady answering he wants to place two orders. Lady says she can't take the order. She's busy and the order-taker is on another phone. (Isn't everyone in business an "order taker"???) Customer says, "Just take my phone number in New York (Hauser is in Connecticut) and call me back."

"I don't know if I can do that. Let me see how long the order-taker will be busy." Silence for a full minute. [Couldn't she have taken the order in the same amount of time? Or the phone number?]

Now the order-taker gets on the phone. When the customer gives his name, she knows him, doesn't have to ask for the credit card number; knows it's on file; thanks the Customer for the order, says good-bye using the customer's first name!

QUESTION: Why not:
(1) Immediately take the customer's phone number as he requests and call him back? A phone cost of less than a dollar for a $50 order . . .

(2) Or, take the order quickly if it's a simple one, if he's on file. Why irritate ANY customer by not responding to what is asked?

Training tip: When the phone rings, it could be a request for information, a complaint or an order. If it's an order— BOOK IT!

BIG BUYER

Tower Records—NYC

Tower advertised special sale discounts on all classical CDs. Customer typed a *five-page* list of CDs he wanted, called Tower, got to a supervisor who would not take the list over the phone nor assign a salesperson. "Our salespeople are not on commission!" (That's an explanation??)

Next day, the customer went to the store, gave the list to a clerk who collected the huge list of CDs, put them in two big shopping bags and then added up the prices. The total was $543. (The average Tower sale is $15.) And . . . the clerk had to be reminded to price the five-page total at the special advertised sale discount.

The customer put the bags of CDs in his car, parked the car, locked it and returned to find the car broken into and the bags of CDs gone.

Next day, back to Tower. Big Buyer seeks out the supervisor, tells him about the theft ("check with the police if you want"), and asks that the order be replaced at the discount prices of yesterday. (The four-day sale had ended the day before.) Ready? *The supervisor refused to fill the $543 order at the discount prices* which the customer was prepared to pay for again (pending the insurance company refund).

(Are there "non-intelligence" tests for salespeople like this?)

CASH & CARRY

A man we know sold his condo in the Chicago area, and walked over to Tallman Savings and Loan carrying $40,000 in cash. (Without a bodyguard?)

He entered the bank and stood in line. As usual, the line moved slowly. He stood, inched forward, and was finally at the window.

"I'd like to deposit this money (plunking down the impressive stash on the teller's counter) and—"

"You're in the wrong line for deposits. You'll have to go over there . . ." said the idiot teller pointing to a distant window.

Inhaling one deep, deep breath of disbelief, our friend slowly exhaled, "OOOkay, if that's what you say," and walked out. That's O-U-T. A $40,000 WAYMISH looking for someone to take its money.

WHAT'S SPECIAL ABOUT YOU?

A PLACE TO PUT YOUR PURSE

A WELL-TO-DO MAN and his wife were visiting Vienna's lavish and luxurious Imperial Hotel—certainly among the world's finest. As they were being seated at a table in their restaurant, a waiter silently approached and placed a small low table to the left of the wife's chair. "For your purse, Madam." He bowed and retreated to a waiting position.

Yes, the man thought. That's always a problem for women. Does the purse go on the floor? Will someone stumble on it? Should she hang it on the back of the chair? Excellent touch of service, he mused.

Like all of us of a certain age, the man's wife needed glasses to read the menu. As she began quietly fishing in her purse for glasses, the waiter magically reappeared bearing an ornately decorated leather box.

Intrigued, the man watched as the waiter removed the cover and revealed about 30 pairs of spectacles, each carefully couched in velvet slots!

As his wife removed a pair of spectacles, the man wondered why more elegant hoteliers (if that's what you call hotel owner-operators), haven't toured Europe to discover these peaks of elegant attention to travelers.

True, few of us have seen this ultra level of posh service, but consider the lesson. How few managements think beyond the ordinary. The exceptional ones carefully "walk through" every step the customer will take in dealing with their business. Then they create interesting solutions that the customer appreciates.

Beware of All Fads

By following the group or imitating a leader, you'll always be second best and too late. If you're not the leader in a category, *start a new category*. Think as a contrarian, figure out what your customers really want, and how you can best give it to them at a profit.

In the steel fabricating business, 50 companies bid on a standard structural steel job. Usually, the winning bidder was either one of the giant producers or a firm that made a bidding error. The better answer for the smaller supplier was to get out of the straight bidding wars and develop a niche expertise where customers paid for design, delivery and experience.

Customers choose between competing suppliers based on their *sense of value*. Value equals quality . . . relative to price. Quality includes all the non-price attributes in the product and service. You don't have to be off the chart, just be able to offer a superior combination of quality, price and value. Be special.

Why You're Special

Three questions that may help you define it.

What's your market uniqueness?

_____

_____

Why do customers want to do business with you?

_____

_____

Define your uniqueness in a way that everyone can understand.

_____

_____

THE FINISHING TOUCH

Max Grassfield, an upscale men's clothier in Denver's Cherry Creek section, anticipates just about everything a customer can ask for. He offers free parking, early-morning side-door entry—with coffee waiting. A free shoeshine stand. Removal of spots. Buttons sewn on. Custom patterns when the next time Max's buyers go to the New York market.

His salesmen, who have been with Max for years, know the customers. Shoe bags with every pair of shoes purchased. A marvelously detailed computer information bank of customers' sizes, birthdays, anniversaries, wife's name, how the customer should be addressed (formally or informally) and a small package containing a shoe horn, extra collar stays, and a traveler's shoeshine puck as a going-away gift. Appropriately, the shine puck has a slogan: "The Finishing Touch," tastefully inscribed on top.

Never satisfied, Max constantly challenges himself and his salesmen with "What else can we do for Grassfield customers?"

PUTTING IT ALL TOGETHER

The Bombay Company started as a furniture catalog store, mailing from Canada in 1973. Opened a retail store in New Orleans, and has expanded to over 400 stores in the U.S. and Canada.

An attractive, brightly-polished, dark wood CD cabinet was staring out from the shiny catalog pages and drew us to one of their local outlets. The salesmen were coated and tied. Helpful. Polite. Reserved. The atmosphere was more like a fine jewelry store than a furniture shop (shoppe).

"We'll take it—this one," pointing to the handsome floor sample CD rack. The credit card was swiped, the voucher signed, and then the news came, "We'll put the pieces in your carton in a moment."

Pieces? Carton? It comes unassembled? Whoa, wait a minute . . . please. With age comes some wisdom. Wisdom dictates that there are people skilled with their hands, artful in figuring out diagrams, artisans who just naturally can put things together. Not in this household.

Sad experience and large repair bills have taught immediate and shameless admission of No Talent for this kind of thing. Our slogan with furniture, plumbing or repair is, "Call The Man!"

So our buyer summons his most helpless look, admits complete ineptness and urges the manager to give special permission and please deliver a finished, all-together piece of furniture.

The manager listens, judges the contrite purchaser, and agrees. "Come back in half an hour and we'll have it ready, but please understand, we do not ordinarily do this." Of course. Yes. Fine. Anything you say.

Happily back in 45 minutes, the shining assembled mahogany rack awaits. Macho Man Purchaser hoists the CD holder to his shoulder, wades through the mall and rides up the escalator to the sidewalk valet area. A sharp-eyed parking attendant says, "Excuse me, sir, one of those shelves is in backwards, see?" and he points to a middle cross bar. Damn if it isn't.

"You bought this at Bombay, yes?" he smiles. Yes. "They are very nice people. Why don't you leave it here with me and go ask them if they can handle this here instead of carrying it all the way back to the store, no? OK, don't worry. I'll watch it."

He watches. I go. With an "Oh my," Darryl, the Bombay manager, summons his stockroom clerk and instructs him to get his tools along with several yards of wrapping gauze. "Go upstairs with this gentleman and fix his shelf, there." At the valet sidewalk, Paul, the stockroom man, begins disassembling and reassembling the three-shelf rack in full view of waiting, intrigued parking-area patrons.

The sharp-eyed valet captain periodically comes by to supervise the work. "Ah—good," he says. "Doing OK." [What would we do without his supervision?]

Finally we (that is Paul) are finished. We shake hands. He is thanked profusely. And tipped generously. (No talent, you pay.)

QUESTION: Have you heard of any retail store lately that was willing to stretch like this to satisfy a $130 purchase?

We haven't. And frankly, I think there are two or three Bombay items I saw that will make great Christmas gifts.

COME SEE US, Y'HEAR?

"Service station" is mainly an oxymoron—a self-canceling description, but not so at K&S, a local Mobil station.

There, both Sarkis and Greg know how to keep customers. Pull in to get gas and Sarkis comes out of his garage. He wipes his hands, shakes your hand, smiles and says, "Hello, dear—a little coffee to start the day?" inviting you to share his private coffee bar—even though he and Greg have coffee-for-sale at their mini-mart a few steps away.

And when son Chris's aged VW van wouldn't start, Sarkis asks, "Where is it?" Hearing it was in the parking lot at our office, he shrugged, "Sunday when I go to church I'll take a look." He did, left a note, "You can move it now. I fixed the gas line leak. S." And the charge? No, just another shrug and, "No big deal, come have coffee."

When daughter Lisa came to visit from San Francisco, her car would go, stop, go, stall. She eventually got stuck in the shopping district. Sarkis went off with a pocket full of tools, got the car going, did an adjustment and smiled broadly at her, "Hey, if you need some gas, you know where to come."

QUESTION: With gas stations on every third corner and frantic sign-switching of gasoline prices every few days, where do we stop—even though K&S is a few blocks further east than we ordinarily travel? You betcha!

Lifetime Value of a Customer. What's it worth? K&S knows.

NOT WHERE—JUST *WHICH*?

There's a tire store chain in the Pacific Northwest—Les Schwab Tires.

They have some 360-plus outlets covering Washington, Idaho, Oregon (maybe Northern California and /or other states).

Once you have bought a tire from Les Schwab, you're a Les Schwab Customer—no matter where you are.

I had a flat in Medford— went to a Les Schwab place (I bought the tires in Portland). The tire is fixed and put back on the truck, the spare is where it belongs in ten minutes—no charge—just, "Is there anything else we can do for you?"

Jackie Akre, my secretary, couldn't get her car started one noon-time. The battery cables were corroded beyond repair. I helped get her car started, told her to go to the nearest Les Schwab and buy a new bat-tery—they would fix the cables.

She went to the local Les Schwab and told them the story. They checked the battery and told her it did not need to be replaced yet, then fixed her cables. No charge—just "Have a Nice Day!" This took ten minutes and Jackie is not even a customer—but she will be.

When it's time to replace my car or truck tires, the only decision I have to make is *which* Les Schwab do I go to?

The only thing wrong with Les Schwab—they only have tires, bat-teries, shocks and suspensions. Now, if they did engines and transmis-sions, there would be no need to take my car anywhere else—ever!

Building Your Own Legend:
A Preview to Carl Sewell's Service

From the customer's point of view . . .

(A) How well is our problem-solving operation working?
    [Survey and Discover!]
(B) How fast and reliably do we respond to a customer's problem?
    [Ask customers, not our people!]
(C) What else can we do to satisfy our customers?
    [Use Focus groups! Accept, then analyze *all* ideas.]

From an Internal Point of View . . .
(A) Do we learn from our recurring problems?

[Check your WAYMISH reports.]
(B) Or are we fixing the same problem over and over?
[Ask "Who's seen this happen before?"]
(C) Can our employees admit there *is* a problem without fear
of punishment?
[This could be the beginning of a new era]
(D) Are our people rewarded for helping solve our company
problems?
[Yes or No. Not "Maybe."]

We suggest you review these points after reading the
abbreviated "Legend of Carl Sewell" below.

Carl Sewell owns a bunch of car agencies, headquartered in Texas.
His passion for customer service and anti-WAYMISH programs has
become legendary.

Some of his ideas and philosophies can be used in any business:
(1) Finding out *what the customer really wants* . . .
(2) Moving the answers "up front"—before the problems start!
(3) Price is rarely the way to win customers—somebody can
always undersell you.

Carl Sewell decided to find out what his car buyers liked and
didn't like—the WAYMISHes, you might say. So he asked his
customers. (Novel idea, huh?)

Not surprisingly, customers told him the things that annoyed them
most were . . . limited service hours, employee rudeness, undepend-
able repairs, inconvenience in not having transportation while their car
was being serviced and, a major complaint—surprises in billing.

Sewell addressed the annoyances and pledged longer hours,
employee training and the creation of a customer feedback system with
answers before the customer left the agency.

He also committed to doing the repair job right the first time, and
providing car loaners while service or repairs were done.

One of his most ingenious innovations was *purposely overestimat-
ing* repairs by a percentage and then charging less! But then Sewell

went beyond these standard customer peeves to make it easier and more pleasant to do business with him.

Sewell car buyers aren't charged for services he describes as "Would you charge a friend for this?" Like what? Replacing a broken key; flat-tire repair being available at any time. Another touch—customers have salespeoples' home phone numbers. Need a battery charge in an airport parking lot—on a Sunday night? You got it! (What are friends for?)

Finally, when something goes wrong, Sewell's people fix it fast and with a smile. His philosophy—If Sewell's service rate is 99% and you have 1,000 customers a month, the 1% of the time when you fail a customer may mean little *statistically*, but to those ten customers, you have failed 100 percent.

Apologize—no excuses—fix the problem. Keep the customer! (Sound familiar now?)

Finally, Sewell learns from mistakes. If a repair job has to be redone, all the people involved examine the process: the technician who worked on the car and the supervisor who gave the instructions both look into where and why the problem arose.

"What you inspect becomes what you expect" is the motto—chasing down the reasons for failure sends a loud message that doing the job right the first time is critical.

How many of Sewell's ideas can you adapt to your business?

Of course the solution is to "Think out-of-the-box," do something different and that's what happened in this anti-WAYMISH tale.

Get the customer what he wants—even if you don't stock or serve that item. Story: Outstanding clothing store in Alabama. Good customer needs winter coat to travel north. Wasn't stocked in this store but they promise delivery. Store went to competitor, bought coat at retail, replaced label with their store label, solved the situation, didn't make a dime on this transaction . . . but (all together now) *kept the customer!*

It's called **Building a Customer for Life.**

OUR CONCLUSION

MANAGERS OFTEN THINK they have to browbeat employees into a positive customer mode, so they're surprised that we advocate "selling" customer-orientation to employees.

Studies show that one of the key factors in keeping good employees is their perception that the company is providing good, honest service to customers.

You don't have to convince most employees about the value of anti-WAYMISH behavior—you just have to make it clear that serving customers is the company's first priority, and that, as employees, they are the critical factor in delivering the service. *Show* them how to do it, *let them know* how they're doing and then *trust them* to perform.

So it really is imperative that you and your business learn to seek out and identify the WAYMISH viruses in your operation and wage a continual campaign to stamp them out.

Unfortunately, WAYMISHes are like bamboo, you stamp it out here . . . cut it there and it creeps underground to appear . . . over there. In another department. In shipping. Billing. Mishandling incoming calls. Nothing monstrous. Just small insidious mistakes. Often all but invisible.

You have to look hard. Check carefully. Peer into every nook and cranny of your Customer Service corners.

The WAYMISH is there—believe it!

Admittedly.... no one has a lockup on the definitive answer to the never-ending problems of Customer Service. Our contribution is creating the term, "WAYMISH."

We hope you and your company will adopt "WAYMISH" as the password to identify these nearly invisible, constantly recurring, customer-irritating fumbles that all people in contact with customers make—sooner or later.

Beware also of the WAYMISH created by insensitive systems.

And we hope even more fervently that this same "WAYMISH" word will be a definite signal to you that there *are* attitudes, responses and reactions to your customers that need correcting and training.

AFTERWORD

Three things happened after we published this book . . .

1. From phone calls, letters and personal comments from customers and meeting planners, it was clear that the word "WAYMISH" has entered the language and is now a short hand signal to identify any mistake in Customer Service. People use it as a verb, too: "I've been Waymished."

2. After reading the book, a number of business leaders realized they needed to reexamine their *total* Customer Service training. Executives admitted to "forgetting" some of their departments where WAYMISH could attack—accounting, collection, billing, delivery, in-bound telephone, checkout procedures.

In fact, they agreed it is necessary to send the anti-Waymish message to *any* employee who had *any* contact with customers in any way. It makes good business sense to have all employees and management trained in *Keeping the Customer.*

3. Many of these companies, like Liquid Controls (IL), Neutron Industries (AZ), Classic Hotels (Norway), Grappone Auto (NH), use stories from the WAYMISH book as a dramatic way to instill the importance of "WAYMISH Prevention." Employees see and hear the seemingly insignificant mistakes that can cause that fearful phrase, "I'm never going to do business with these people again!"

As a Result

Companies have ordered quantities of books and distributed them as training tools for their management staff, their regional and local managers. Advance Auto, headquartered in Roanoke, VA, went one step further: every person promoted in their organization now gets a copy of WAYMISH.

Present Tense

So, we have progressed from "just a book" to being able to provide an unusual training tool. We are sending a Training Guide and a sheet called Great Ideas with every book shipment. The Training Guide will explain very simply how to use the book's stories to best advantage in short, weekly meetings by asking employees to solve the mistakes reported in sections of the book. This generates involvement and companies find that nearly all their employees learn and remember by creating better answers for the book's WAYMISH situations.

The Great Ideas (courtesy of Cary Zucker of Neutron) shows you a fast and foolproof way to collect ideas on the spot, immediately, before they're forgotten, by supplying easels and markers, or note pads at employees' work stations. Reviewing ideas in a short time frame and recognizing employee contributions has raised morale and generated a number of innovative ideas for his and other companies using Great Ideas.

If you'd like samples of either the Training Guide and/or Great Ideas, just fax, send a note, or call toll free 1 888 WAYMISH (929-6474). To order additional books, use the same number.

A BOW AND THANKS TO

Our very special thanks to each of you generous contributors for your true-to-life stories—and congratulations to you for being an active member of the First Battalion of **"WAYMISH WARRIORS"**!

Karen Applebome
Bob Ayrer
Keith Bailey
Joe Balli
The Bauman Brothers
Warren Bennis
Jimmy Bernard
Stephen Birmingham
Louise Borchert
Sharon Hanes Brown
Jim Buckley
Dale Byrne
Wade Lee Cannon
Frank Cardulo
Jan Carlzon
Clay Carr
Brian Clewer
Isabel Claire Cohen
Don Cohn
Jeff Comment
Betty Considine
Christopher Considine

Lisa Considine
Carol Christison
Paul DeLaCourt
Helen Dennis
Sara Dooley
Peter Drucker
Steve Merrill Durham
Dr. Alice Ginott
Max Grassfield
Arthur Greene
Bill Hall
Gary Hall
Irwin Helford
Clem Hellmann
Lee Iacocca
Mike Lamberti
Stew Leonard
Richard Lochridge
Jeff Maitles
Bob Manroe
Stanley Marcus
David Meister

Sue Mitchell
Lane Moore
Jeff Newby
Christopher Norton
Rudy Oetting
Bill Osborn
Joan Pajunen
Dan Pappalardo
Arch Parker
Gene Pepper
Janis and Dick Pollen
Tony Pompeo
Feargal Quinn (Dublin, Ireland)
Terri Radek
Murray Raphel
Jim Rhode
Dewey Richardson
Robert Richland
Mrs. Robaledo
Warren Rubin
Betsy Sanders
Carl Sewell
Louis Shackett
John Sheehan
John Shiner
Karl Otto Skogland
Jim Smith
Phil Thorpe
Sarkis Tomajin
Lila Wallace (Reader's Digest)
George Walters
Bill & Phyllis Webster
Norton Weinstein
Mary Wilson
Barbara Young
George Zahka
Cary Zucker

Construction Equipment News
Consumer Reports
The Economist

The Great Brain Robbery
Harvard Business Review
Los Angeles Times
New York Times
Sloan Management Review (Sloan/Lawler)

And there are stories about...

AirTouch Cellular
America West Airlines
American Airlines
American Express
AT&T
Avis
Bag City
Balduccis (LA)
Bank of New York
Barnes & Noble
Barnett Banks
Bendix of Canada
Bergdorf Goodman
The Bombay Company
Budget Rent a Car
Claremont Diner
CRM Films
Dell Computers
Dodsworth Restaurant
Doubletree Hotels
Eddie Bauer
Federal Express
Four Seasons Hotels
Gracious Home
GTE
Hallmark
Hauser Chocolates
Helzberg Jewelry
The Hill Companies
Horchow
The Hotel Carlyle
Houlihans
Hyatt Hotels

Il Fornaio Restaurant
Intel (Pentium)
J. Peterman Catalogs
J.C. Penney
Joe's Stone Crab
L.L. Bean
La Quinta
Land's End
Les Schwab Auto
Magpies
Marriott Hotels
McCormick &
  Schmick's Restaurant
Merit Cleaners
Metropolitan Museum
  of Art
Muscolino Inventory
  Services
North Face
Neutron Industries
Nordstrom Department
  Stores
Paragon Sporting Goods
Patagonia
Delia Price
Puritan Clothing
Republic Savings
Ritz Carlton Hotels
Saks Fifth Avenue
SAS Airlines
SAS Hotel Denmark
Bernie Schleifer
Shearson Lehman
Sheraton Boston
South New England
  Telephone Co.
Southwest Airlines
Taco Bell
Tallman Savings
Target Stores
Tower Records
Toys R Us

Trane
TWA
United Airlines
United States Postal
  Service
Viking Business Products
The Wiz
Xerox

Special thanks to Susan Hall and Allana Barton for their heroic and enthusiastic support: selecting, organizing, typing and editing.

And a huge vote of gratitude to Mary "Fitz" Fitzpatrick who saved us from grammatical and "parseimonius" disgrace with her apt editing, canny changes and admirable advice.

To Alex Swart who racked his creative designer brain to create a snazzy cover to explain the funny word WAYMISH.

Plus, Delia Price, whose sharp eye and strict adherence to the *Gregg Manual* saved many a slip 'twixt the proofing and printing.

And finally to Bernie Schleifer who has been at the bottom of the funnel from the beginning, winnowing, sorting, suggesting and producing a book we hope he is as proud of as we are.

ABOUT THE AUTHORS

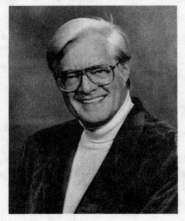

RAY CONSIDINE, is a respected national speaker on Sales and Customer Service. He's been described as the "Dean of Sales Trainers" by his clients and recently was complimented as "a salesman's salesman."

He deals with the real stuff—not academic bromides. Doesn't stay at the podium. Walks the aisles, remembers names and audiences immediately pick up the feeling he is "one of them."

His experience with decades of hands-on selling with major corporations, utilities, construction and finance is what makes his presentations different. And practical.

Considine is Irish—a gifted storyteller—which guarantees your audience will not only learn, but laugh and remember the word pictures and images he uses long after your meeting is over.

For information on fees and availabilities call Toll Free: 1-888-929-6474
Considine & Associates
#1125 Gateway Tower
3452 E. Foothill Blvd, Pasadena CA 91107
Phone: (626) 795-4282   Fax: (626) 795-5892
E mail: raycon1@rayconsidine.com
web site: www.rayconsidine.com

TED COHN is one of the country's leading consultants on closely-held companies. Combining a B.A. from Harvard with an M.A. in psychology from Columbia, he was a director of a children's camp, an executive in a family steel business, managing partner of a regional CPA firm, and has consulted with hundreds of companies on strategy, marketing, succession, financial planning, personnel and compensation.

As a speaker and writer he has produced over 20 books and tapes, 400 articles, and has presented about 1,000 speeches and seminars to trade associations and professional groups from A to Y—American Management Association to Young Presidents Organization.

Concerned with supporting managers who want to work at higher levels of accountability and objectivity, Ted has initiated and served on many advisory committees and boards of directors of private and public companies.

Currently, he helps companies in these continuing relationships to focus on their unique human resource and marketing capabilities—the essence of the WAYMISH story.

Ted can be reached at 923 Fifth Avenue (4A), New York, NY 10021-2649. Phone and fax: (212) 517-6671. E mail: aliceted@compuserve.com

How'd You Do?

Score one point for each "yes" answered

	Yes	No
Do you know what percentage of your customers you keep each year?	_____	_____
Do you know what percentage of your customers you lose each year?	_____	_____
Do you know the top three reasons your customers leave?	_____	_____
Do you know what your customers' #1 service expectation is?	_____	_____
In the last three months have you personally contacted at least ten former customers to find out why they quit you?	_____	_____
Do you understand what the life-time value of your customer is?	_____	_____
Do you have written customer service quality standards?	_____	_____
Do you articulate your customer service quality standards in understandable and measurable terms to employees and customers?	_____	_____
In the last six months have you checked to see if any of your customers' expectations have changed?	_____	_____
Do you know how many members of your staff serve internal vs. external customers?	_____	_____
Are any of your customer service performance standards tied in with incentive programs?	_____	_____
Is everyone in the organization required to take a minimum number of hours of Customer Care training programs annually?	_____	_____

IF YOU SCORED: YOU ARE:

12	A CSQ* Legend
10 - 11	A CSQ* Star
7 - 9	Jo(e) Average
4 - 6	Benchwarmer
Below 4	In the Penalty Box

CSQ = Customer Sensitivity Quotient

How do *you* score?

Working Relationships, Boca Raton, Florida, JoAnna Brandi

<table>
<tr><td>

3
WAYS
TO
ORDER

</td><td>

Phone...
Toll free: 1-888-WAYMISH
(1-888-929-6474)

Fax...626-795-5892

Mail...WAYMISH
#1125 Gateway Tower
3452 E. Foothill Blvd
Pasadena CA 91107-6009

</td></tr>
</table>

W.A.Y.M.I.S.H.

Why Are You Making It So Hard...
for me to give you my money
by Ted Cohn and Ray Considine
192 pages Paperback $16.00

One minute's lousy service and you lose a customer for life! Make it EASIER for your customers to give you their money. Learn how to detect and stamp out the WAYMISH "bug" in your business.

The Great Brain Robbery:

How to Steal Ideas and use them
by operating "Out of the Box"
by Ray Considine
and Murray Raphel
220 pages Hardback $17.00

One of those "keeper" books for any business. A terrific collection of ideas on selling, merchandising and promotion.

Quantity discounts and combination orders available. Please call toll free for information.

_____ **WAYMISH** copies @ $16.00 + (CA tax 1.30/ea) = $_____

_____ **Brain Robbery** copies @ $17.00 + (CA tax 1.65/ea) = $_____

TOTAL $_____

METHOD OF PAYMENT:

☐ Check enclosed payable to WAYMISH
☐ Billing for larger orders can be arranged. Please call: 1-888-929-6474.
☐ Yes! Send us the free Training Guide and Great Thoughts mini-manual with our order.

Xerox This Order Form and fax to 626-795-5892

NAME _____

NAME OF BUSINESS _____

STREET ADDRESS _____

CITY _____ STATE _____ ZIP _____

PHONE _____ E-MAIL_____ FAX _____

Additional charges for rush orders or international orders.

USE THE OTHER SIDE OF THIS PAGE TO ORDER ADDITIONAL BOOKS.

Be sure to check box for the Free Training Guide!

• • •

Waymish is available as a powerful, fast-paced 60 or 90 minute Customer Service Workshop as part of your next meeting or convention

Call toll free 1-888-"WAYMISH" — 929-6474